Retiring to Italy

The Complete Guide to Living Your Italian Dream

Jefferson Foster

Disclaimer

It is crucial to note that while this book aims to provide a comprehensive overview of retiring to Italy, the author is not a tax expert, legal professional, or licensed financial advisor. The information presented in this book is for general educational and informational purposes only and should not be considered as professional advice.

Tax laws, legal requirements, and financial regulations can be complex and are subject to change. Every individual's situation is unique, and what works for one person may not be appropriate for another. Therefore, it is strongly recommended that anyone considering a move to Italy should obtain professional tax, legal, and immigration advice tailored to their specific circumstances.

Contents

Introduction

La Dolce Vita - Your Guide to Retiring in Italy

As the sun-drenched hills of Tuscany roll out before you, their undulating slopes adorned with silvery olive groves and orderly vineyards, you can't help but feel a sense of wonder and possibility. The distant tolling of church bells mingles with the cheerful chatter emanating from a nearby piazza, where locals gather for their daily ritual of espresso and conversation. This is Italy - a land where history and modernity intertwine seamlessly, where art and culture are not mere pastimes but integral parts of daily life, and where the pursuit of beauty and pleasure is elevated to an art form. It is in this enchanting setting that you find yourself contemplating a bold and exciting prospect: retirement in Italy.

The allure of Italy as a retirement destination is as multi-faceted as the country itself. For many, it begins with the images that have captivated travelers for centuries: the grandeur of Rome's ancient monuments, the romantic canals of Venice, the Renaissance splendor of Florence, and the breathtaking beauty of the Amalfi Coast. These iconic scenes have fueled countless dreams of a life steeped in history, art, and natural beauty. But the appeal of Italy runs far deeper than these postcard-perfect vistas.

Introduction

At its heart, the dream of retiring in Italy is about embracing a way of life - the famed "dolce vita" (the sweet life) that prioritizes quality over quantity, savoring over rushing, and connection over isolation. It's about waking up each morning to the aroma of freshly baked bread wafting from the local bakery, spending leisurely afternoons exploring winding medieval streets or sipping wine in sun-dappled piazzas, and ending each day with a meal that celebrates the bounty of the land and the joy of good company. It's about immersing yourself in a culture that values family, friendship, and community, where neighbors become friends and every interaction is an opportunity for warmth and connection.

For many retirees, Italy represents an opportunity to slow down and rediscover the pleasures of a simpler life. In a world that often seems to move at an ever-accelerating pace, Italy offers a refreshing alternative - a place where taking time to enjoy life's small pleasures is not just accepted but expected. Whether it's lingering over a long lunch with friends, taking an evening passeggiata (stroll) through town, or simply sitting in a cafe and watching the world go by, Italy encourages a pace of life that allows for true appreciation and enjoyment.

The Italian approach to food and dining is a prime example of this philosophy. Here, meals are not merely about sustenance but are central to the rhythm of daily life and the fabric of social connections. From the morning ritual of cappuccino and cornetto to the elaborate Sunday lunches that bring families together, food in Italy is a celebration of both flavor and community. For retirees, this offers not just the pleasure of world-renowned cuisine but also a way to connect with local culture and build relationships within their new community.

Italy's rich cultural heritage is another powerful draw for retirees. Few places in the world offer such a concentration of art, architecture, and historical sites. Living in Italy means having some of the world's greatest artistic and architectural treasures right at your doorstep. Whether you're passionate about Renaissance art, fascinated by ancient Roman history, or simply appreciate beautiful design, Italy offers

Introduction

endless opportunities for exploration and learning. Many retirees find that living among such beauty and history provides constant inspiration and opportunities for personal growth.

The country's natural beauty is equally compelling. From the snow-capped peaks of the Alps to the crystal-clear waters of the Mediterranean, Italy offers a diversity of landscapes that cater to a wide range of preferences and lifestyles. Whether you dream of a rustic farmhouse in the Tuscan countryside, a seaside villa on the Italian Riviera, or an apartment in a bustling city center, Italy has a setting to match your ideal retirement vision. The mild Mediterranean climate in much of the country is an added bonus, allowing for an outdoor lifestyle and year-round enjoyment of nature.

For many retirees, the prospect of learning a new language and immersing themselves in a different culture is part of the excitement of moving to Italy. While the idea of mastering Italian may seem daunting at first, many find that the process of learning the language opens up new neural pathways, keeping the mind sharp and engaged. Moreover, the daily interactions involved in learning and practicing Italian provide countless opportunities for forming connections and deepening your understanding of the culture.

Italy's healthcare system is another factor that makes it an attractive retirement destination. The country boasts a high-quality public healthcare system that is accessible to legal residents, complemented by a private system for those who prefer additional options. Many retirees find that they have access to excellent medical care, often at a lower cost than in their home countries. The Italian approach to healthcare, which often emphasizes prevention and holistic well-being, aligns well with the needs and priorities of many retirees.

The cost of living in Italy, while varying significantly between regions, can be surprisingly affordable, especially when compared to major cities in North America or Northern Europe. While popular tourist destinations and large cities like Rome, Florence, and Milan can be expensive, many smaller towns and rural areas offer a high quality of

Introduction

life at a much lower cost. This can allow retirees to stretch their retirement savings further, enjoying a lifestyle that might be out of reach in their home countries.

However, it's important to note that retiring in Italy is not without its challenges. Navigating the country's infamous bureaucracy, adapting to cultural differences, and managing the logistics of an international move all require patience, flexibility, and careful planning. That's where this book comes in. "La Dolce Vita: Your Guide to Retiring in Italy" is designed to be your comprehensive companion as you plan for and transition into your Italian retirement.

In the chapters that follow, we'll take you on a journey through all aspects of retiring in Italy, from the dreaming and planning stages to the practicalities of daily life and long-term considerations. We'll begin by exploring the various regions of Italy, helping you understand the unique characteristics and offerings of each area to aid in your decision of where to settle. From the sun-baked hills of Sicily to the fashionable streets of Milan, each region of Italy has its own distinct flavor, and finding the right fit for your lifestyle and preferences is crucial to a successful retirement.

We'll then dive into the nitty-gritty of making your Italian retirement dream a reality. We'll guide you through the often complex process of obtaining the necessary visas and residency permits, helping you understand the legal requirements for retiring in Italy. This includes navigating the bureaucratic processes, understanding the different types of visas available, and ensuring you meet all the criteria for legal residency.

Financial planning is a crucial aspect of any retirement, and even more so when retiring abroad. We'll provide a comprehensive overview of the financial considerations involved in retiring to Italy, including understanding the cost of living in different areas, managing your income and investments across international borders, and navigating the Italian tax system. We'll also discuss healthcare costs and insurance

Introduction

options, helping you plan for both routine and unexpected medical expenses.

Finding the right home is another critical step in your Italian retirement journey. Whether you're looking to rent or buy, we'll guide you through the process of house hunting in Italy. We'll discuss the pros and cons of different types of properties, from city apartments to rural villas, and provide insights into the Italian property market. We'll also cover the legal aspects of property ownership in Italy, including the roles of notaries and other professionals involved in property transactions.

Healthcare is often a primary concern for retirees, and we'll dedicate a full chapter to understanding the Italian healthcare system. We'll explain how to access both public and private healthcare services, discuss the quality of care available in different regions, and provide guidance on health insurance options for expatriates. We'll also touch on wellness and preventive care practices in Italy, helping you maintain your health and vitality throughout your retirement years.

Integrating into Italian society is key to a fulfilling retirement experience, and we'll provide plenty of advice on how to become part of your new community. We'll discuss strategies for overcoming language barriers, building social connections, and embracing Italian customs and social norms. We'll also explore opportunities for volunteering, joining clubs and associations, and participating in local events and festivals.

Daily life in Italy has its own unique rhythms and customs, and we'll help you navigate these with confidence. From understanding shop opening hours and banking practices to mastering the art of Italian coffee culture, we'll provide practical tips for managing everyday tasks and embracing the Italian way of life. We'll also delve into the joys of Italian cuisine, offering guidance on shopping in local markets, dining out, and even trying your hand at Italian cooking.

Italy's rich cultural heritage offers endless opportunities for leisure and recreation, and we'll explore these in depth. We'll discuss how to make the most of Italy's world-class museums, art galleries, and historical sites, as well as how to enjoy its natural beauty through activities like hiking, cycling, and beach-going. We'll also look at opportunities for continued learning and personal growth, from language classes to art workshops and beyond.

While the prospect of retiring in Italy is undoubtedly exciting, it's important to approach it with a clear understanding of the challenges as well as the rewards. We'll provide an honest look at the potential difficulties you may face, from dealing with bureaucratic hurdles to managing long-distance family relationships. We'll offer strategies for overcoming these challenges and maintaining a positive outlook throughout your transition.

Finally, we'll look at long-term considerations for your Italian retirement. This includes estate planning and legal considerations, strategies for staying connected with your home country, and tips for adapting your lifestyle as you age. We'll also discuss options for accessing support services and long-term care, should the need arise.

Throughout the book, we'll share real-life stories and insights from expatriates who have successfully made the transition to retirement in Italy. Their experiences - both the triumphs and the challenges - will provide valuable perspectives and practical advice to help you on your own journey.

"Retiring to Italy- The Complete Guide to Living Your Italian Dream" is more than just a practical handbook - it's an invitation to embrace a new chapter in your life, one filled with beauty, culture, and the joy of discovery. Whether you're drawn to Italy for its art and history, its natural beauty, its celebrated cuisine, or simply the allure of a more relaxed and pleasure-filled way of life, this book will help you turn your retirement dreams into reality.

As you embark on this journey, remember that retiring in Italy is not just about changing your address - it's about embracing a new way of life. It's about waking up each day to new adventures, whether that

Introduction

means exploring a medieval hill town, perfecting your pasta-making skills, or simply savoring an espresso in your local piazza. It's about challenging yourself to learn and grow, to form new friendships, and to see the world from a different perspective.

The path to retiring in Italy may not always be smooth, but for those who make the journey, the rewards are immeasurable. From the moment you wake up to the sound of church bells and the aroma of fresh bread, to the evening hours spent sipping wine and watching the sun set over terracotta rooftops, life in Italy offers a richness and depth of experience that many find transformative.

As we guide you through the practicalities of making your Italian retirement a reality, we encourage you to keep sight of the dream that brought you to this point. Let the beauty of Italy - its art, its landscapes, its people - inspire you. Let the warmth of Italian hospitality embrace you. Let the rhythms of Italian life remind you to slow down, to savor, to truly live.

Your Italian retirement adventure is waiting. With this book as your guide, you're well-equipped to navigate the challenges and embrace the joys that lie ahead. So take a deep breath, say "si" to new experiences, and prepare to embark on the journey of a lifetime. Benvenuti in Italia - welcome to Italy, and welcome to your new life of la dolce vita.

It is crucial to note that while this book aims to provide a comprehensive overview of retiring to Italy, the author is not a tax expert, legal professional, or licensed financial advisor. The information presented in this book is for general educational and informational purposes only and should not be considered as professional advice.

Chapter 1
Dreaming of Italy

Italy has long captured the imagination of travelers, artists, and dreamers from around the world. Its rich history, stunning landscapes, vibrant culture, and unparalleled cuisine have made it a top destination for tourists and expatriates alike. But for those considering retirement, Italy offers something even more enticing: the promise of la dolce vita – the sweet life. In this chapter, we'll explore the myriad reasons why Italy stands out as an exceptional choice for retirees and take a journey through its diverse regions, each offering its own unique blend of attractions and lifestyles.

The decision to retire abroad is not one to be taken lightly, but for many, Italy represents the ideal culmination of a lifetime of hard work and dreams. Picture yourself waking up each morning to the gentle tolling of church bells, stepping out onto a sun-drenched terrace overlooking rolling hills covered in vineyards, or strolling through ancient cobblestone streets on your way to a local café for your morning espresso. These daily pleasures, so integral to the Italian way of life, are just the beginning of what makes Italy an irresistible retirement destination.

One of the primary draws of Italy for retirees is its rich cultural heritage. Few countries can boast such a concentration of art, architecture, and historical sites spanning millennia. From the ruins of ancient Rome to the Renaissance masterpieces of Florence, from the Byzantine splendors of Ravenna to the Baroque excesses of Sicily, Italy offers an unparalleled opportunity to immerse oneself in the history of Western civilization. For retirees with a passion for art and history, the ability to explore world-renowned museums, magnificent churches, and archaeological sites at leisure is nothing short of a dream come true.

Consider the possibility of spending your retirement years wandering through the Vatican Museums, gazing up at Michelangelo's frescoes in the Sistine Chapel, or standing before Leonardo da Vinci's Last Supper in Milan. Imagine having the time to truly appreciate the intricate mosaics of Ravenna's early Christian monuments or to explore the ancient ruins of Pompeii at your own pace. In Italy, history is not confined to museums; it's an integral part of daily life, visible in the architecture of every town and city, in the traditions that have been passed down through generations, and in the stories told by locals over a glass of wine.

But Italy's cultural offerings extend far beyond its museums and monuments. The country's vibrant traditions, festivals, and customs provide endless opportunities for engagement and discovery. Whether it's participating in local sagre (food festivals) celebrating regional specialties, witnessing the pageantry of historical reenactments, or simply observing the daily rhythms of life in a small town, retirees in Italy find themselves constantly enriched by new experiences and insights into a culture that values connection, tradition, and the art of living well.

Imagine being part of the vibrant atmosphere of Venice's Carnevale, with its elaborate masks and costumes, or experiencing the excitement of Siena's Palio, a bareback horse race that dates back to medieval times. Picture yourself joining in the grape harvest celebrations in wine regions across the country or participating in the olive oil pressing festivities in rural communities. These events are not just spectacles for tourists; they're living traditions that offer retirees a chance to become part of the fabric of Italian cultural life.

Speaking of living well, Italy's renowned cuisine is another major attraction for potential retirees. The country's culinary traditions vary widely from region to region, offering a lifetime's worth of gastronomic exploration. From the hearty, truffle-infused dishes of Piedmont to the seafood-rich fare of the Amalfi Coast, from the simple, rustic flavors of Tuscan cooking to the complex, Arab-influenced cuisine of Sicily, Italian food is a never-ending source of pleasure and discovery. For retirees, the opportunity to shop in local markets, learn traditional recipes, and savor long, leisurely meals with friends and family represents a fundamental shift in lifestyle – one that prioritizes quality, freshness, and the joy of shared experiences.

In Italy, food is more than sustenance; it's a way of life, a source of pride, and a means of connecting with others. Retiring in Italy means having the time to truly appreciate this aspect of the culture. You might find yourself learning to make pasta from scratch under the guidance of a local nonna, or discovering the subtle differences between olive oils pressed from different varietals of olives. You could spend mornings browsing bustling farmers' markets, selecting the ripest tomatoes and the freshest herbs for your evening meal. The emphasis on seasonal, local ingredients not only results in delicious meals but also fosters a deeper connection to the rhythms of nature and the local community.

Closely tied to Italy's food culture is its wine heritage. With twenty distinct wine-growing regions producing everything from world-famous Barolos and Brunellos to lesser-known but equally delightful local varietals, Italy is a paradise for wine enthusiasts. Many retirees find great pleasure in exploring the country's numerous wine routes, visiting vineyards, and developing a deeper appreciation for the artistry and tradition behind Italian winemaking. The ability to enjoy a glass of excellent local wine with every meal – often at prices far lower than one would pay abroad – is just one of the many small luxuries that make retirement in Italy so appealing.

For those with a passion for oenology, retirement in Italy offers the chance to delve deep into the world of wine. You might find yourself attending wine tastings led by passionate sommeliers, learning about the unique characteristics imparted by different terroirs, or even volunteering during the vendemmia (grape harvest) at a local vineyard. Many retirees in wine regions like Tuscany or Piedmont develop friendships with local winemakers, gaining insider knowledge about the best vintages and hidden gem wineries that tourists rarely discover.

Italy's natural beauty is another compelling reason to consider it as a retirement destination. From the snow-capped peaks of the Alps and Dolomites in the north to the sun-drenched beaches of the south, from the rolling hills of Tuscany and Umbria to the dramatic coastlines of Liguria and the Amalfi Coast, Italy offers an incredible diversity of landscapes. This variety not only provides stunning backdrops for daily life but also offers endless opportunities for outdoor activities. Retirees can enjoy hiking, skiing, swimming, boating, or simply basking in the beauty of their surroundings. The country's abundant natural hot springs, many of which have been developed into luxurious spa resorts, offer additional opportunities for relaxation and rejuvenation.

Imagine spending your retirement years exploring the hiking trails of the Cinque Terre, with its colorful coastal villages perched dramatically above the Mediterranean. Picture yourself skiing in the Dolomites in winter, then returning to the same area in summer for spectacular mountain hikes. You could spend leisurely days sailing along the Amalfi Coast, or exploring the unique landscapes of regions like Tuscany's Val d'Orcia or Sicily's Mount Etna. For nature lovers and outdoor enthusiasts, Italy offers a lifetime's worth of exploration and adventure.

The Italian climate, while varying from region to region, is generally mild and pleasant, making it ideal for retirees seeking to escape harsh winters or oppressive summers. The Mediterranean climate that predominates in much of the country is characterized by hot, dry summers and mild, wet winters – perfect for those who enjoy spending time outdoors year-round. Even in the northern regions, where winters can be colder, the climate is generally less severe than in many parts of North America or Northern Europe.

This favorable climate contributes significantly to the quality of life for retirees in Italy. It allows for an outdoor-oriented lifestyle, with many opportunities for al fresco dining, leisurely walks, and outdoor social gatherings. The abundance of sunshine not only lifts the spirits but also contributes to the growth of the fresh produce that is so integral to Italian cuisine. For those coming from colder climates, the ability to enjoy outdoor activities and natural beauty throughout most of the year can be a revelation, contributing to both physical and mental well-being.

For many retirees, the pace and quality of life in Italy are perhaps the most attractive aspects of relocating there. Italians are famous for their commitment to enjoying life, valuing leisure time, and nurturing social connections. The concept of "dolce far niente" – the sweetness of doing nothing – encapsulates an approach to life that many retirees find deeply appealing after years of career-driven hustle. In Italy, long lunches, afternoon siestas, and evening passeggiate (leisurely strolls) are not indulgences but essential components of a well-lived life.

This slower pace extends to all aspects of daily living. Shopping in small, specialized stores rather than impersonal supermarkets becomes a social activity as much as a chore. Meals are events to be savored, not rushed through. Friendships are cultivated over years of shared coffees, meals, and conversations. For retirees accustomed to the frenetic pace of modern life, this shift can be both challenging and deeply rewarding, offering a chance to rediscover the pleasures of a simpler, more connected way of living.

In Italy, you might find yourself spending an hour each morning at your local café, sipping espresso and chatting with neighbors. Your grocery shopping might involve visits to the baker for fresh bread, the greengrocer for locally grown produce, and the butcher for expertly prepared meats – each stop an opportunity for conversation and connection. Evenings might be spent in the town square, joining friends and neighbors for the ritual of the passeggiata, where the community comes together to stroll, socialize, and enjoy the cooler air of the evening.

The sense of community in Italy, particularly in smaller towns and villages, is another draw for many retirees. Unlike in some countries where retirees might feel isolated or disconnected, Italian culture places a high value on social connections across all age groups. Older individuals are respected for their wisdom and experience, and it's not uncommon to see multiple generations socializing together in piazzas, cafes, and at community events. For expatriate retirees, this welcoming atmosphere can make the process of integration much smoother and more enjoyable.

Many retirees find that they quickly become part of their local community, invited to family dinners, included in holiday celebrations, and welcomed into local social circles. This sense of belonging can be particularly valuable for those who are far from their own families. It's not uncommon for retirees to develop close relationships with their neighbors, shopkeepers, and even the local barista, creating a support network that enhances their quality of life and sense of security.

Italy's healthcare system is another factor that makes it an attractive retirement destination. The country boasts a high-quality, affordable public healthcare system that is consistently ranked among the best in the world. While navigating the system can be challenging for non-Italian speakers, many retirees find that the quality of care they receive far exceeds what they might expect in their home countries, often at a fraction of the cost. Additionally, Italy's emphasis on preventive care and overall wellness aligns well with the priorities of many retirees.

The Italian approach to healthcare is holistic, focusing on overall well-being rather than just treating symptoms. Many retirees appreciate the personal attention they receive from doctors, who often take the time to discuss lifestyle factors and preventive measures. The abundance of fresh, healthy food, the emphasis on walking and staying active, and the generally lower stress levels associated with the Italian lifestyle all contribute to better health outcomes for many retirees.

The cost of living in Italy, while varying significantly from region to region, can be surprisingly affordable, especially when compared to major cities in North America or Northern Europe. While popular tourist destinations and large cities like Rome, Florence, and Milan can be expensive, many retirees find that they can enjoy a high quality of life in smaller towns or rural areas at a much lower cost. Fresh, high-quality food, excellent wine, and many cultural activities are often more affordable in Italy than in other Western countries, allowing retirees to indulge in the pleasures of Italian life without breaking the bank.

It's important to note that while some aspects of life in Italy can be very affordable, others may be more expensive than what retirees are accustomed to. Utilities, for example, can be costly, and imported goods often come with a premium price tag. However, many retirees find that by embracing the local lifestyle – shopping at markets, eating seasonally, and enjoying local entertainment – they can live well on a modest budget.

Now that we've explored some of the general reasons why Italy is an appealing retirement destination, let's take a closer look at the various regions of the country and what they offer to retirees. Italy is divided into 20 regions, each with its own distinct character, traditions, and attractions.

Starting in the north, we find the regions of Valle d'Aosta, Piedmont, Liguria, and Lombardy. Valle d'Aosta, nestled in the Alps, offers breathtaking mountain scenery and excellent skiing. It's perfect for retirees who love outdoor activities and cooler climates. The region's strong French influences are evident in its bilingual status and unique cuisine, offering a fascinating cultural blend.

Piedmont, known for its sophisticated capital Turin, its wine country (home of Barolo and Barbaresco), and its truffle-rich cuisine, appeals to food and wine enthusiasts. The region's elegant cities, with their grand cafes and museums, offer a high quality of urban life, while its countryside provides opportunities for peaceful rural living. The annual Alba White Truffle Fair is a major draw for gourmands from around the world.

Liguria, with its stunning coastline known as the Italian Riviera, offers a perfect blend of seaside living and historic charm in towns like Portofino and Cinque Terre. The region's mild climate makes it popular with retirees seeking year-round outdoor living. Its cuisine, featuring pesto and focaccia, is renowned throughout Italy.

Lombardy, home to the fashion capital of Milan and the beautiful Lake District including Lake Como, provides a mix of urban sophistication and natural beauty. For retirees seeking a cosmopolitan lifestyle with easy access to nature, Lombardy offers the best of both worlds. The region's economic strength means excellent infrastructure and healthcare facilities.

Moving east, we encounter the regions of Trentino-Alto Adige, Veneto, and Friuli-Venezia Giulia. Trentino-Alto Adige, with its dramatic Dolomite mountains and Austrian influences, is ideal for retirees who enjoy outdoor activities and a touch of Central European culture. The region's bilingual nature (Italian and German) and unique autonomy make it a fascinating cultural enclave.

Veneto, home to Venice, Verona, and charming hill towns, offers an intoxicating mix of art, history, and natural beauty. From the canals of Venice to the vineyards that produce Prosecco, Veneto offers diverse experiences for retirees. The region's strong economy and excellent transportation links make it practical as well as beautiful.

Friuli-Venezia Giulia, bordering Slovenia and Austria, is known for its unique cultural blend, excellent wines, and beautiful, uncrowded beaches. For retirees seeking a less touristy experience with a strong local culture, this region offers much to discover. Its location makes it an excellent base for exploring Central Europe as well as Italy.

In central Italy, we find Emilia-Romagna, Tuscany, Umbria, Le Marche, Lazio, and Abruzzo. Emilia-Romagna is a food lover's paradise, home to Parma ham, Parmigiano-Reggiano cheese, and Bologna, Italy's culinary capital. The region's strong economy, excellent healthcare, and high quality of life make it attractive to retirees, while its location in the heart of Italy makes travel convenient.

Tuscany, perhaps the most famous region among foreign retirees, offers the quintessential Italian experience with its Renaissance cities, medieval hill towns, and iconic countryside. From the art treasures of Florence to the vineyards of Chianti, Tuscany offers endless opportunities for cultural enrichment and beautiful living. However, its popularity means that some areas can be expensive and crowded with tourists.

Umbria, often called the "green heart of Italy," provides a quieter, more affordable alternative to Tuscany, with equally beautiful landscapes and rich history. Towns like Assisi and Perugia offer cultural riches, while the countryside provides opportunities for peaceful rural living. The region's central location makes it convenient for exploring other parts of Italy.

Le Marche, stretching from the Apennine Mountains to the Adriatic Sea, is a hidden gem offering diverse landscapes and charming towns at reasonable prices. For retirees seeking an authentic Italian experience away from mass tourism, Le Marche offers much to discover, from its beautiful beaches to its medieval hill towns.

Lazio, dominated by Rome, offers the excitement of the Eternal City as well as beautiful countryside and coastal areas. For retirees who want access to world-class cultural attractions while still having the option of a more relaxed lifestyle, Lazio provides an excellent balance. The region's transportation links make it easy to explore the rest of Italy and Europe.

Abruzzo, with its mix of mountains and coastline, is gaining popularity among retirees for its natural beauty, affordable real estate, and traditional way of life. Often described as "the greenest region in Europe," Abruzzo offers opportunities for both seaside and mountain living. Its relatively undiscovered status means that retirees can find excellent value for money here.

Southern Italy and the islands each offer unique experiences, from the vibrant culture of Naples in Campania to the baroque beauty of Lecce in Puglia, from the ancient ruins of Sicily to the pristine beaches of Sardinia. These regions often provide a more relaxed, affordable lifestyle, though sometimes with fewer amenities than the north.

Ultimately, the choice of where to retire in Italy depends on your personal preferences, budget, and desired lifestyle. Whether you dream of city life or rural tranquility, seaside relaxation or mountain adventures, there's a corner of Italy that's perfect for you.

As you contemplate retiring in Italy, remember that it's not just about finding the perfect location. It's about embracing a new way of life, challenging yourself to grow, and opening your heart to the transformative power of la dolce vita. The journey may have its challenges, but for those who take the leap, the rewards of retiring in Italy can be immeasurable.

Are you ready to make your Italian retirement dream come true?

Chapter 2
Legal Essentials

As you embark on your Italian retirement journey, understanding the legal landscape is crucial. This chapter will guide you through the maze of visas, residency requirements, and essential documentation needed to make your dream of retiring in Italy a reality. While the process may seem daunting at first, with proper preparation and knowledge, you can navigate these legal waters with confidence.

Understanding Italian Visa Requirements

The first step in your legal journey to retiring in Italy is obtaining the appropriate visa. For non-EU citizens, including Americans, Canadians, and Britons post-Brexit, a visa is necessary for stays longer than 90 days. The visa most relevant for retirees is the Elective Residence Visa (Visto per Residenza Elettiva), often referred to as the retirement visa.

The Elective Residence Visa is designed for individuals who wish to reside in Italy and can support themselves financially without working.

This makes it ideal for retirees who have a pension, retirement savings, or other passive income sources. It's important to note that this visa strictly prohibits any form of employment in Italy, whether paid or unpaid.

To be eligible for the Elective Residence Visa, you must meet several criteria:

1. Financial Resources: You must demonstrate that you have sufficient financial means to support yourself without working in Italy. The exact amount required can vary, but it's generally recommended to show a minimum annual income of €31,000 for a single person or €38,000 for a couple. This income should come from pensions, property rentals, investments, or other passive sources.
2. Accommodation: You need to prove that you have arranged for a place to live in Italy. This can be either a property you've purchased or a long-term rental agreement.
3. Health Insurance: You must have comprehensive health insurance coverage valid in Italy.
4. Clean Criminal Record: A certificate showing no criminal record is required.
5. Passport: Your passport should be valid for at least three months beyond your planned stay in Italy.

The application process for the Elective Residence Visa begins at the Italian embassy or consulate in your home country. It's crucial to start this process well in advance of your planned move, as it can take several months to gather all necessary documents and receive approval.

When applying for the visa, you'll need to submit a variety of documents, including:

- Completed visa application form
- Recent passport-sized photographs

- Valid passport
- Proof of financial resources (bank statements, pension documentation, etc.)
- Proof of accommodation in Italy
- Comprehensive health insurance policy
- Police clearance certificate
- Letter explaining your reasons for moving to Italy and your plans during your stay

It's important to note that requirements can vary slightly depending on the specific Italian consulate handling your application. Always check with your local Italian consulate for the most up-to-date and specific requirements.

Once your visa is approved, it will typically be valid for one year. This allows you to enter Italy and begin the process of obtaining your residency permit, which we'll discuss in more detail later in this chapter.

Navigating the Permesso di Soggiorno

After arriving in Italy with your Elective Residence Visa, your next crucial step is to apply for a Permesso di Soggiorno (Permit of Stay). This document is essential for legally residing in Italy beyond the initial validity of your visa.

You must apply for the Permesso di Soggiorno within 8 days of arriving in Italy. This tight timeline can be challenging for new arrivals, so it's wise to familiarize yourself with the process before you leave your home country.

The application process for the Permesso di Soggiorno involves several steps:

1. Obtain the application kit: You can get this from a post office (Poste Italiane) that offers the "Sportello Amico" service. The

kit includes the application form and a list of required documents.

2. Complete the application: Fill out the form carefully. Any errors can lead to delays or rejection.
3. Gather necessary documents: These typically include:
   - Copy of your passport and visa
   - Proof of accommodation
   - Proof of financial means
   - Four passport-sized photographs
   - Revenue stamp (Marca da Bollo)
   - Proof of health insurance
4. Submit the application: Return to the post office to submit your completed application and pay the required fees. You'll receive a receipt with the date of your appointment at the Questura (police headquarters).
5. Attend the appointment: At the Questura, you'll provide fingerprints and present original copies of your documents.
6. Collect your Permesso di Soggiorno: After processing, which can take several weeks to a few months, you'll be notified when your permit is ready for collection.

The initial Permesso di Soggiorno for retirement is typically valid for one year. Subsequent renewals can be for two years, provided you continue to meet the requirements.

It's crucial to start the renewal process well before your current permit expires. The renewal application should be submitted at least 60 days before the expiration date to ensure continuity of your legal status in Italy.

Establishing Residency in Italy

Once you have your Permesso di Soggiorno, the next step is to establish official residency in your Italian comune (municipality). This process is known as iscrizione anagrafica (registration of residency).

To register as a resident, you'll need to visit the Anagrafe (registry office) of your local comune. The documents typically required include:

- Valid Permesso di Soggiorno
- Passport
- Codice Fiscale (Italian tax code)
- Proof of accommodation (property deed or rental contract)
- Self-declaration of sufficient financial means

The process of establishing residency usually involves a visit from the local police to verify that you indeed live at the address you've provided. Once your residency is confirmed, you'll receive a certificate of residency (Certificato di Residenza) and can apply for an Italian identity card.

Establishing residency is an important step as it allows you to access various services and benefits, including registering with the national health service (Servizio Sanitario Nazionale) and obtaining an Italian driver's license.

Understanding the Codice Fiscale

The Codice Fiscale is the Italian tax code, similar to a Social Security number in the United States. It's an essential document that you'll need for various aspects of life in Italy, including opening a bank account, signing a rental agreement, and registering for healthcare.

You can obtain a Codice Fiscale from the local office of the Agenzia delle Entrate (Italian Revenue Agency) or through the Italian consulate in your home country before you move. The process is relatively simple and requires only your passport and a completed application form.

Healthcare Registration

Italy's public healthcare system, the Servizio Sanitario Nazionale (SSN), is highly regarded and available to legal residents. As a retiree with a valid Permesso di Soggiorno, you have the option to register with the SSN.

To register, you'll need to visit your local Azienda Sanitaria Locale (ASL) office with the following documents:

- Permesso di Soggiorno
- Codice Fiscale
- Certificate of Residency
- Passport

There is an annual fee for joining the SSN, which varies depending on your income. Once registered, you'll receive a health card and can choose a primary care doctor.

Alternatively, you may choose to maintain private health insurance. In fact, comprehensive health coverage is a requirement for your visa and Permesso di Soggiorno. If you opt for private insurance, ensure that your policy provides adequate coverage for your needs in Italy.

Dealing with Taxes

Understanding your tax obligations is crucial when retiring to Italy. As a resident, you'll be subject to Italian taxes on your worldwide income. However, Italy has tax treaties with many countries, including the United States, to prevent double taxation.

The Italian tax system can be complex, and rates can be high, particularly for higher earners. It's strongly recommended to consult with a commercialista (accountant) who specializes in expatriate taxes to ensure you're meeting all your obligations and taking advantage of any applicable deductions or credits.

Some key points to be aware of:

1. Tax Residency: You're generally considered a tax resident if you're registered as a resident in Italy and spend more than 183 days per year in the country.
2. Worldwide Income: As a tax resident, you're required to declare your worldwide income to Italian authorities.
3. Foreign Assets: You must declare any foreign financial assets through the RW form as part of your annual tax return.
4. Property Taxes: If you own property in Italy, you'll be subject to property taxes (IMU and TASI).
5. Inheritance Tax: Italy has inheritance tax, which can affect how you plan your estate.

Given the complexities of international taxation, it's crucial to seek professional advice to ensure you're compliant with both Italian tax law and the tax laws of your home country.

Buying Property in Italy

Many retirees dream of owning a home in Italy, whether it's a city apartment, a rural farmhouse, or a coastal villa. While non-EU citizens are allowed to purchase property in Italy, there are some important considerations and steps to be aware of:

1. Codice Fiscale: You'll need this to purchase property.
2. Preliminary Contract (Compromesso): This initial agreement sets out the terms of the sale and is legally binding.
3. Notary (Notaio): A notary is required to handle the deed transfer. They will conduct necessary checks on the property.
4. Property Taxes: Be prepared for various taxes and fees, including registration tax, land registry tax, and notary fees.
5. Ongoing Costs: Consider property taxes, utilities, and maintenance costs.

It's highly recommended to work with a reputable real estate agent and a lawyer who specializes in property transactions for foreign buyers. They can guide you through the process and help you avoid potential pitfalls.

Driving in Italy

As a retiree in Italy, you may wish to drive. Non-EU licenses are generally valid for one year from the date of obtaining residency. After this, you'll need to obtain an Italian driver's license.

Italy does not have license exchange agreements with many non-EU countries, which means you may need to take both the theory and practical driving tests to obtain an Italian license. These tests are in Italian, so language proficiency is necessary.

If you bring a car from your home country, you'll need to register it in Italy within 60 days of establishing residency. This process can be complex and costly, so many expatriates find it simpler to sell their foreign car and purchase a vehicle in Italy.

Banking and Finance

Opening an Italian bank account will make many aspects of your life in Italy easier, from paying bills to receiving pension payments. To open an account, you'll typically need:

- Passport
- Codice Fiscale
- Permesso di Soggiorno
- Proof of Address

Some banks offer accounts specifically designed for non-residents or new arrivals, which can be easier to open initially.

When it comes to receiving pension or investment income from abroad, be aware of currency exchange rates and transfer fees. Some retirees find it beneficial to use specialized forex services for large transfers to get better rates than those offered by banks.

Language Considerations

While not strictly a legal requirement, having at least a basic grasp of Italian will make navigating the legal and administrative aspects of your move much easier. Many official forms and processes are only available in Italian, and while larger cities may have English-speaking staff in some offices, this is less common in smaller towns.

Consider taking Italian language courses before your move and continuing your studies once in Italy. Not only will this help with practical matters, but it will also enrich your overall experience of living in Italy.

Staying Informed of Changes

Immigration laws and processes can change over time. It's important to stay informed about any updates that might affect your status or requirements. Regularly check the website of the Italian Ministry of Foreign Affairs and International Cooperation, and consider joining expatriate groups or forums where such information is often shared and discussed.

Seeking Professional Help

Given the complexities of Italian bureaucracy and the importance of getting things right, many retirees find it beneficial to seek professional assistance. Immigration lawyers, tax advisors, and relocation services can provide invaluable help in navigating the legal landscape.

While these services come at a cost, they can save you time, stress, and potentially costly mistakes. When choosing professionals to assist you, look for those with experience helping expatriates, and don't hesitate to ask for references.

Embracing the Process

As you work through these legal requirements, remember that each step brings you closer to your dream of retiring in Italy. Yes, the process can be bureaucratic and at times frustrating, but it's also part of your transition to Italian life.

Try to approach each interaction, each form, each visit to a government office as an opportunity to practice your Italian, to learn more about your new home, and to connect with the people who will be your new neighbors and fellow community members.

Many retirees find that going through this process gives them a sense of accomplishment and a deeper appreciation for their new home. It's a rite of passage that every expat goes through, and it often leads to amusing stories and shared experiences with other foreign residents.

Navigating the legal essentials of retiring to Italy may seem daunting, but with proper preparation and patience, it's entirely manageable. Remember, millions of people have successfully made this journey before you.

By understanding the visa requirements, residency processes, health-care system, tax obligations, and other legal considerations, you're laying a solid foundation for your new life in Italy. Each document you obtain, from your Elective Residence Visa to your Permesso di Soggiorno to your Italian identity card, is a stepping stone on your path to la dolce vita.

As you work through these processes, keep your dream in mind. Imagine the moment when, with all your paperwork in order, you can finally relax on your Italian terrace, sip a glass of local wine, and know that you've officially become a resident of one of the most beautiful countries in the world.

Retiring to Italy

The journey to retiring in Italy is not just about the destination; it's about the experience of immersing yourself in a new culture, navigating challenges, and growing as an individual. Embrace every step of the process, and soon enough, you'll find yourself living the retirement you've always dreamed of in your new Italian home.

Chapter 3
Financial Planning

As you embark on your Italian retirement adventure, one of the most crucial aspects to consider is your financial plan. The dream of sipping espresso in a sun-drenched piazza or strolling through ancient cobblestone streets can quickly become a reality with careful financial planning. This chapter will guide you through the intricacies of budgeting for retirement in Italy, understanding the cost of living across various regions, navigating the Italian tax system, and managing your finances from abroad. By the end of this chapter, you'll have a comprehensive understanding of the financial landscape you'll be entering, allowing you to make informed decisions and ensure a comfortable retirement in your chosen Italian paradise.

Let's begin by discussing the cost of living in Italy. It's important to note that the cost of living can vary significantly depending on the region and whether you choose to live in a city, town, or rural area. Generally speaking, northern Italy tends to be more expensive than the south, and major cities like Rome, Milan, and Florence have a higher cost of living compared to smaller towns or rural areas. However, even within these generalizations, there can be significant variations.

Retiring to Italy

In the north, cities like Milan and Venice are known for their high costs, particularly when it comes to housing. A modest apartment in the center of Milan, for example, can easily cost €1,500 to €2,000 per month in rent. However, if you move to a smaller city in the north, such as Bologna or Verona, you might find rents for similar apartments ranging from €700 to €1,200. The trade-off, of course, is that larger cities often offer more amenities, better public transportation, and potentially more expatriate communities, which some retirees find appealing.

Central Italy, including Tuscany and Umbria, has become increasingly popular with foreign retirees over the years, which has driven up prices in some areas. Cities like Florence and Siena can be quite expensive, with costs similar to those in Milan. However, if you venture into smaller towns or rural areas in these regions, you can find more afford-able options. A farmhouse in the Tuscan countryside might cost anywhere from €200,000 to €500,000 to purchase, depending on its size, condition, and exact location. Renting in these areas can range from €500 to €1,000 per month for a modest apartment or small house.

Southern Italy, including regions like Puglia, Calabria, and Sicily, generally offers a lower cost of living. This can be particularly appealing for retirees on a tighter budget. In these areas, it's possible to find apartments for rent in the €400 to €800 range, even in larger towns. Property prices for purchase can also be significantly lower, with small apartments or townhouses available from as little as €50,000 in some areas. However, it's important to consider that these regions may have less developed infrastructure and fewer expatriate communities, which could present challenges for some retirees.

When budgeting for your Italian retirement, it's crucial to consider all aspects of daily life, not just housing costs. Food costs in Italy can be quite reasonable, especially if you shop at local markets and eat seasonally. Many retirees find that they spend less on food in Italy than they did in their home countries, thanks to the abundance of fresh, local produce and the emphasis on home cooking. A couple might expect to spend anywhere from €300 to €500 per month on groceries, depending on their habits and preferences.

Dining out is an integral part of Italian culture, and many retirees look forward to exploring the local culinary scene. Prices can vary widely depending on the type of establishment and location. A simple lunch of pizza or pasta at a local trattoria might cost €10 to €15 per person, while a more elaborate dinner at a nicer restaurant could run €30 to €50 per person or more. It's worth noting that many restaurants offer a "menu del giorno" or daily fixed-price menu, which can be an excellent value.

Transportation costs are another factor to consider in your budget. If you plan to live in a city with good public transportation, you might find that you don't need a car at all. Monthly passes for public transportation in most Italian cities range from €30 to €50. However, if you prefer to have a car, especially if you're living in a more rural area, you'll need to factor in the costs of purchase or lease, insurance, fuel, and maintenance. Car insurance in Italy can be quite expensive, often running €1,000 or more per year, depending on the type of car and your driving history.

Healthcare is a significant consideration for many retirees. As we discussed in the previous chapter, you have the option to register with the Italian National Health Service (Servizio Sanitario Nazionale or SSN) once you have your residency permit. The annual fee for this varies based on income but is generally around €400 to €2,000 per year. This provides access to Italy's public healthcare system, which is generally of high quality, especially for serious health issues. However, many expatriates choose to maintain private health insurance in addition to or instead of SSN coverage. Private health insurance costs can vary widely based on your age, health status, and the level of coverage you choose, but you might expect to pay anywhere from €2,000 to €4,000 per year for a comprehensive policy.

Utilities are another important budget item. The cost of electricity, gas, water, and waste disposal can vary depending on your location and usage, but a couple might expect to pay €150 to €250 per month for these services. Internet and mobile phone plans are generally afford-able in Italy, with basic packages starting around €20 to €30 per month each.

Entertainment and leisure activities are an essential part of enjoying your retirement in Italy. Costs for these can vary widely depending on your interests and lifestyle. Museum entries typically range from €10 to €20, though many museums offer free or reduced entry days. A cinema ticket might cost €8 to €12. If you enjoy sports, gym member-ships can range from €30 to €80 per month, depending on the facility and location.

When it comes to budgeting for your Italian retirement, it's wise to build in a buffer for unexpected expenses and fluctuations in currency exchange rates. Many retirees find that they need at least €1,500 to €2,000 per month per person to live comfortably in most parts of Italy, though this can vary based on lifestyle choices and location. Some manage on less, while others spend considerably more.

Now, let's delve into the intricacies of the Italian tax system, as under-standing your tax obligations is crucial for effective financial planning. As a resident of Italy, you'll be subject to Italian income tax on your worldwide income. This means that any pension, investment income, or other earnings you receive, regardless of their source, may be taxable in Italy.

The Italian income tax system, known as IRPEF (Imposta sul Reddito delle Persone Fisiche), is progressive, with rates ranging from 23% for income up to €15,000 to 43% for income over €75,000 (as of 2021). However, it's important to note that these rates can change, and there are various deductions and credits that can reduce your overall tax burden.

One significant consideration for many retirees is how their pension income will be taxed. Italy has tax treaties with many countries, including the United States, United Kingdom, and Canada, which can affect how your pension is taxed. In some cases, your pension may be taxed in your home country, in Italy, or split between the two, depending on the specific treaty and the type of pension. It's crucial to consult with a tax professional who is familiar with both Italian tax law and the tax laws of your home country to understand your specific situation.

In addition to income tax, there are several other taxes you should be aware of. If you own property in Italy, you'll be subject to property taxes. The main property tax is IMU (Imposta Municipale Unica), which is calculated based on the cadastral value of the property and varies by municipality. There's also a service tax called TASI, though in many cases, this has been incorporated into the IMU. If you're renting, these taxes are typically paid by the property owner, but it's worth confirming this when you sign your rental agreement.

Another tax to be aware of is the IVAFE (Imposta sul Valore delle Attività Finanziarie all'Estero), which is a wealth tax on financial assets held outside of Italy. This applies to bank accounts, investments, and other financial instruments held abroad. The rate is 0.2% of the value of these assets, with a minimum tax of €34.20 per account.

Italy also has an inheritance tax, which is something to consider in your long-term financial planning. The rates and exemptions vary depending on the relationship between the deceased and the heir, ranging from 4% to 8%, with substantial exemptions for close family members.

Given the complexities of the Italian tax system and its interaction with international tax laws, it's highly recommended to work with a commercialista (Italian accountant) who specializes in expatriate taxation. They can help you navigate the system, ensure you're meeting all your obligations, and potentially find ways to optimize your tax situation legally.

Managing your finances from abroad is another crucial aspect of retiring in Italy. One of the first steps you'll want to take is opening an

Italian bank account. This will make it easier to pay bills, receive pension payments, and manage your day-to-day expenses. Most major Italian banks offer accounts suitable for expatriates, and some international banks have branches in Italy, which can make the transition easier.

When choosing a bank, consider factors such as the availability of English-speaking staff, online banking options, and fees for international transfers. Some banks offer special accounts for pensioners that may have reduced fees or other benefits. It's also worth investigating whether your home country bank has any partnerships with Italian banks, as this could simplify the process of transferring funds or opening an account.

Managing your investments from abroad requires careful consideration. Depending on your situation, you may choose to keep some investments in your home country while moving others to Italy. It's important to be aware that as an Italian resident, you'll need to declare all foreign financial assets on your annual tax return, even if they don't generate income.

For many retirees, a significant portion of their income comes from pensions or retirement accounts in their home country. You'll need to decide whether to have these payments sent directly to your Italian bank account or keep them in an account in your home country and transfer funds as needed. This decision can depend on factors such as exchange rates, transfer fees, and tax implications.

If you're receiving payments in a foreign currency, you'll need to consider the impact of exchange rate fluctuations on your budget. Some retirees choose to use specialized forex services for large transfers to get better rates than those offered by banks. Others may consider hedging strategies to protect against currency risk, though this requires careful consideration and potentially professional advice.

It's also worth noting that as a resident of Italy, you may be subject to restrictions on certain types of investments or financial products that you were able to use in your home country. For example, some U.S. mutual funds are not available to residents of European Union countries due to regulatory differences. This is another area where professional advice can be invaluable.

As you plan your finances for retirement in Italy, it's crucial to consider the long-term sustainability of your plan. This includes not only ensuring that your savings and income will cover your expenses for the duration of your retirement but also considering factors like inflation and potential changes in your health or care needs as you age.

One strategy that many retirees find helpful is to create a detailed budget for their first year in Italy, and then review and adjust it regularly based on their actual experiences. This can help you identify areas where you may be spending more or less than expected and make necessary adjustments.

It's also wise to maintain an emergency fund, perhaps equivalent to six months of expenses, to cover unexpected costs or temporary disruptions to your income. This can be particularly important when living abroad, where you may not have the same support network or understanding of systems as you did in your home country.

Insurance is another important consideration in your financial planning. In addition to health insurance, which we discussed earlier, you may want to consider other types of insurance such as home insurance (which is not mandatory in Italy but can be wise, especially if you own property), liability insurance, and travel insurance for trips outside of Italy.

If you own property in Italy, you'll need to factor in ongoing maintenance costs and potential renovation expenses. Italian properties, particularly older ones, can require significant upkeep. It's wise to budget for regular maintenance as well as set aside funds for larger projects that may be necessary over time.

For those who plan to travel frequently, either back to your home country or to explore other parts of Europe, it's important to build these costs into your budget. While living in Italy puts you in an excellent position to explore Europe, travel costs can add up quickly if not planned for.

As you settle into your new life in Italy, you may find that your spending patterns and priorities shift. Many retirees find that they spend less on material goods and more on experiences, whether that's dining out, attending cultural events, or traveling. Being flexible with your budget and open to these changes can help you make the most of your retirement.

It's also worth considering the potential impact of life changes on your financial plan. This could include things like family members coming to visit or stay for extended periods, changes in your health or mobility, or the possibility of eventually needing to move back to your home country. While it's impossible to predict everything, having contingency plans can provide peace of mind.

One aspect of financial planning that's particularly relevant for expatriate retirees is estate planning. This can be complex when you have assets in multiple countries and are subject to different legal systems. It's advisable to work with legal professionals in both Italy and your home country to ensure that your wishes are properly documented and legally valid in both jurisdictions.

Finally, it's important to stay informed about changes in financial regulations, tax laws, and exchange rates that could affect your situation. Joining expatriate groups or forums can be a good way to stay updated on these issues, as can regularly consulting with financial and tax professionals.

Retiring in Italy is a dream for many, and with careful financial planning, it can be a sustainable and enjoyable reality. By understanding the costs of living, navigating the tax system, managing your finances effectively, and planning for the long term, you can set yourself up for a retirement filled with the best that Italian life has to offer. From savoring long lunches in charming trattorias to exploring ancient historical sites, from immersing yourself in the local community to discovering hidden corners of your new home, your Italian retirement can be a rich and rewarding chapter of your life. With a solid financial foundation, you can focus on embracing the Italian lifestyle, building new relationships, and creating memories that will last a lifetime. Remember, the goal of all this financial planning is not just to survive in Italy, but to thrive – to fully enjoy the culture, beauty, and dolce vita that drew you to this remarkable country in the first place.

Chapter 4
Finding a Home

One of the most exciting aspects of retiring to Italy is finding your perfect Italian home. Whether you dream of a sun-drenched villa in Tuscany, a charming apartment in a bustling city center, or a rustic farmhouse in the rolling hills of Umbria, the process of finding and securing your ideal retirement abode is a journey filled with both challenges and rewards. This chapter will guide you through the intricacies of house hunting in Italy, helping you navigate the decision between renting and buying, understand the Italian property market, and overcome the potential pitfalls that foreign buyers might face.

Let's begin by addressing one of the most fundamental decisions you'll need to make: whether to rent or buy your Italian home. Both options have their merits, and the right choice will depend on your personal circumstances, financial situation, and long-term plans. Renting offers flexibility and can be a good option if you're not yet sure where in Italy you want to settle permanently. It allows you to experience different areas before committing to a purchase, and it frees you from the responsibilities of property ownership such as maintenance and property taxes. Renting can also be a wise choice if you're not planning to stay in Italy indefinitely or if you prefer to keep your capital liquid for other investments.

On the other hand, buying property in Italy can be an excellent long-term investment. Property ownership gives you a sense of permanence and allows you to truly make a place your own. In many parts of Italy, especially in popular tourist areas, property values have shown steady appreciation over time. Owning your home can also provide a sense of security in retirement, knowing that you have a valuable asset and won't be subject to rising rents or the whims of landlords. However, it's important to consider that buying property comes with additional costs and responsibilities, including property taxes, maintenance expenses, and potentially complex legal processes.

If you decide to rent, at least initially, you'll find that the Italian rental market operates somewhat differently from what you might be used to in your home country. Long-term rentals in Italy typically involve a standard contract called a "4+4" contract, which provides an initial four-year term with an automatic renewal for another four years unless either party gives notice. This provides a good degree of security for tenants. However, it's also possible to find shorter-term rentals, especially in tourist areas, though these may come at a premium price.

When looking for a rental property, it's important to work with reputable agencies or landlords. Be prepared to provide proof of income or financial stability, as landlords will want assurance that you can pay the rent. You may also be asked for a security deposit, typically equivalent to one to three months' rent. Always insist on a written contract, even if the landlord suggests a verbal agreement, which is not uncommon in some parts of Italy. Having a written contract protects both parties and clarifies expectations.

If you decide to buy property in Italy, you're embarking on an exciting but potentially complex journey. The Italian property market can be quite different from what you're accustomed to, and there are several unique aspects to be aware of. First, it's important to understand that Italy doesn't have a centralized Multiple Listing Service (MLS) like many other countries. This means that estate agents typically only show properties that they have personally listed, which can limit your options if you work with just one agent. For this reason, many foreign buyers choose to work with multiple agencies to see a wider range of properties.

When you begin your property search, you'll quickly discover that Italy offers a vast array of housing options, each with its own charm and challenges. In cities, you might find yourself choosing between a modern apartment in a newer development or a characterful flat in a historic palazzo. In rural areas, options might range from fully-restored villas to crumbling farmhouses in need of significant renovation. It's crucial to consider not just the aesthetic appeal of a property, but also its practicality for your retirement lifestyle. For instance, that 16th-century townhouse might be incredibly charming, but are you prepared for the potential maintenance issues that come with an older property? Similarly, a remote countryside property might offer peace and stunning views, but how will you feel about the isolation, especially as you age?

One unique aspect of the Italian property market is the prevalence of properties needing renovation. Many foreign buyers are attracted to the idea of purchasing a run-down property at a low price and restoring it to its former glory. While this can be a rewarding project, it's important to approach it with open eyes. Renovation in Italy can be more complex and time-consuming than you might expect, involving navigating local bureaucracy, working with artisans who may have different concepts of time and deadlines, and often uncovering unexpected issues as work progresses. If you're considering a property that needs work, it's wise to get detailed surveys and estimates before committing, and to factor in a significant contingency budget.

As you search for properties, you'll encounter some terminology specific to the Italian market. A "rustico" typically refers to a rural property, often in need of renovation. An "appartamento" is an apartment or flat, while a "villa" usually denotes a detached house, often with a garden. A "casale" is a farmhouse, which might be either restored or in need of work. Pay attention to the stated square meterage of properties, as this is typically the total floor area, including walls, which means the actual living space may be smaller than you expect.

When you find a property you're interested in, it's crucial to do your due diligence. This is where working with a good estate agent and a reputable lawyer becomes invaluable. They can help you navigate the complexities of Italian property law and ensure that the property is legally sound. For instance, they can check that the property has all the necessary permits and certificates, that there are no outstanding debts or liens on the property, and that the stated boundaries and land ownership are accurate.

One peculiarity of the Italian system is the concept of "cadastral value." This is the value assigned to the property for tax purposes, and it's often significantly lower than the market value. While this can result in lower property taxes, it can also cause complications if you later want to sell the property, as capital gains tax is calculated based on the difference between the cadastral value and the sale price.

Once you've found a property you want to purchase, the buying process in Italy typically involves several stages. First, you'll make an offer, which if accepted, leads to the signing of a preliminary contract or "compromesso." This is a legally binding document that outlines the terms of the sale, including the price, any conditions, and the proposed completion date. At this stage, you'll typically be required to pay a deposit of around 10-20% of the purchase price. It's crucial to have a lawyer review this contract before you sign, as backing out after this point can result in the loss of your deposit.

After the compromesso is signed, your lawyer will conduct further checks on the property, including ensuring that there are no planning irregularities or unauthorized building works. This is also the time when you'll need to arrange your financing if you're not paying cash. It's worth noting that while it's possible for non-residents to obtain mortgages in Italy, the process can be more complex and the terms may be less favorable than for Italian residents.

The final stage of the purchase is the signing of the deed of sale or "atto di vendita" in front of a notary. The notary's role is to ensure that all legal requirements have been met and to register the change of ownership. At this point, you'll pay the balance of the purchase price, along with various taxes and fees. These can add up to around 10-15% of the purchase price, so it's important to factor these into your budget from the outset.

Whether you choose to rent or buy, location will be a crucial factor in your decision. Italy's diverse regions each offer their own unique life-style and advantages for retirees. The rolling hills of Tuscany and Umbria have long been favorites among foreign buyers, offering a blend of beautiful landscapes, rich culture, and a relaxed pace of life. However, their popularity means that property prices in these regions can be high, especially in well-known areas like Chianti or around cities like Florence and Siena.

For those seeking a more affordable option, regions like Le Marche, Abruzzo, or Puglia can offer excellent value. These areas are increas-ingly popular with foreign buyers, offering beautiful scenery, authentic Italian experiences, and generally lower property prices. However, it's important to consider factors like accessibility, especially if you plan to travel frequently or expect regular visits from family and friends.

Coastal areas can be appealing for those who love the sea, but it's important to consider the seasonal nature of many Italian seaside towns. While bustling in summer, they can be very quiet in winter, with many businesses closed. This might suit some retirees perfectly, while others might prefer a location with year-round activity.

City living in Italy can offer a vibrant cultural scene and excellent amenities, but often at a higher cost. Apartments in the historic centers of cities like Rome, Florence, or Venice command premium prices, although more affordable options can often be found in peripheral neighborhoods or smaller cities. When considering a city property, pay attention to factors like noise levels, parking availability (if you plan to have a car), and the presence of an elevator if you're looking at upper floor apartments.

Rural properties can offer tranquility and often more space for your money, but come with their own considerations. Access can be an issue, with some properties only reachable via unpaved roads which can become difficult in bad weather. Services like high-speed internet, which many retirees consider essential, may not be readily available in more remote areas. It's also worth considering how comfortable you'll be with a more isolated lifestyle, particularly as you age.

Climate is another important factor to consider when choosing your location. While Italy is generally thought of as having a Mediterranean climate, there's actually considerable variation across the country. Northern regions can have cold winters with snow not uncommon in many areas. Central Italy typically has milder winters but can still experience cold spells. The south and the islands generally have the mildest winters but can have extremely hot summers. Consider how comfortable you are with heat and cold, and how the local climate might affect any health conditions you have.

As you narrow down your search to specific properties, there are several practical considerations to keep in mind. For apartments, check the condominium fees and what they cover. These can vary widely and may include costs for shared facilities like elevators or gardens. For houses, consider the size of the land and whether you're prepared for the maintenance it will require. Many foreign buyers underestimate the work involved in maintaining a large garden or olive grove.

The orientation of the property is also important. In the hot Italian summers, a south-facing property can become uncomfortably warm, while north-facing rooms might feel chilly in winter. Properties with a mix of exposures often offer the best of both worlds. Pay attention to natural light, which can significantly affect your enjoyment of a space, especially during the shorter winter days.

Retiring to Italy

If you're considering an older property, be prepared for some quirks. Many historic Italian homes have thick walls, which can provide excellent insulation but may also make Wi-Fi coverage challenging. Plumbing and electrical systems in older properties may need updating to meet modern standards. Heating can also be an issue, as many older Italian homes weren't designed with central heating in mind. While retrofitting is possible, it can be costly.

For those interested in generating some income from their property, perhaps by renting it out when you're not in residence, it's important to choose a location and property type that will appeal to the rental market. Properties in popular tourist areas or cities with year-round appeal generally offer the best rental potential. However, be sure to check local regulations, as some areas have restrictions on short-term rentals.

Regardless of whether you choose to rent or buy, furnishing your new Italian home can be one of the most enjoyable parts of the process. While you might be tempted to ship all your existing furniture from home, consider embracing the opportunity to adopt a more Italian style. Many retirees find that their tastes change as they settle into Italian life, moving towards a simpler, more relaxed aesthetic that suits the local environment.

Italian furniture stores offer a wide range of options, from sleek modern designs to rustic traditional pieces. For those on a budget, Italy's many antique markets and flea markets can be treasure troves of unique, affordable pieces. In rural areas, you might even find local artisans who can create custom furniture for you, often at prices comparable to mass-produced items.

When furnishing, keep in mind the realities of Italian living. For instance, while air conditioning is becoming more common, it's not universal, so investing in good fans and choosing furniture and textiles that help keep spaces cool can be wise. Similarly, while modern Italian kitchens can be as well-equipped as any in the world, many older properties have smaller kitchens than you might be used to, so choosing space-efficient appliances and storage solutions can be crucial.

As you settle into your new Italian home, whether rented or owned, remember that creating your perfect retirement haven is an ongoing process. Many retirees find that their needs and preferences evolve as they become more immersed in Italian life. The home that seemed perfect at first might reveal limitations over time, or you might discover a different area of Italy that calls to you. This is all part of the adventure of retiring in Italy, and maintaining a degree of flexibility can help you make the most of your experience.

Finding your ideal home in Italy is more than just a practical necessity – it's a key part of realizing your retirement dreams. Whether you end up in a bustling city apartment, a tranquil countryside villa, or a charming coastal retreat, your Italian home will be the base from which you explore your new life. It will be where you host newfound friends for long, leisurely dinners, where you retreat to relax after days of exploring your adopted country, and where you create the memories that will make your retirement years truly special.

The process of finding and securing your Italian home may have its challenges, but with patience, careful research, and the right professional support, you can navigate it successfully. And when you finally turn the key in the door of your own Italian retreat, whether as a renter or an owner, you'll know that you've taken a crucial step in your journey towards la dolce vita. Your Italian home isn't just a place to live – it's the setting for the next exciting chapter of your life, full of new experiences, new friendships, and the incomparable pleasure of truly living the Italian way.

Chapter 5
The Italian Healthcare System

As you embark on your retirement journey in Italy, understanding the country's healthcare system is crucial for ensuring your well-being and peace of mind. Italy boasts a healthcare system that is consistently ranked among the best in the world, offering high-quality care that is generally accessible and affordable. This chapter will guide you through the intricacies of the Italian healthcare system, helping you navigate your options, understand how to access services, and make informed decisions about your health coverage during your retirement years in Italy.

The foundation of healthcare in Italy is the Servizio Sanitario Nazionale (SSN), or National Health Service. Established in 1978, the SSN is based on the principles of universal coverage, solidarity, human dignity, and health needs. It's a regionally based national health service that provides universal coverage to citizens and residents, including eligible foreign residents. The SSN is primarily funded through corporate and value-added tax revenues, which are collected by the central government and then redistributed to the regions. This system ensures that healthcare is available to all, regardless of income or social status, which is a comforting thought for retirees considering a move to Italy.

One of the first things you'll notice about the Italian healthcare system is its regionalized structure. While the national government sets the fundamental principles and goals of the health system, each of Italy's 20 regions is responsible for organizing and delivering health services. This regional approach allows for some flexibility in how healthcare is delivered, but it also means that the quality and efficiency of services can vary from one region to another. As a retiree, this is something to consider when choosing where to settle in Italy. Some regions, particularly in the north, are known for having more efficient and better-equipped healthcare systems, while southern regions may face more challenges in terms of resources and waiting times.

To access the public healthcare system as a retiree in Italy, you'll need to register with the SSN. This process, known as iscrizione al Servizio Sanitario Nazionale, is typically done after you've obtained your residence permit (permesso di soggiorno). To register, you'll need to visit your local health authority office, known as the Azienda Sanitaria Locale (ASL). You'll need to bring your valid ID, residence permit, and Italian tax code (codice fiscale). There is an annual fee for joining the SSN, which varies depending on your income. As of 2021, this fee ranges from about €387.34 to €2,788.86 per person. Once registered, you'll receive a health card (tessera sanitaria) and can choose a primary care doctor from a list provided by the ASL.

It's important to note that while EU citizens can use their European Health Insurance Card (EHIC) for temporary stays, if you're retiring in Italy, you'll need to register with the SSN for comprehensive coverage. For non-EU citizens, including Americans and post-Brexit British citizens, private health insurance is typically required to obtain a visa and residence permit. However, once you have your residence permit, you have the option to register with the SSN.

Once you're registered with the SSN, you'll have access to a wide range of services. These include visits to your primary care doctor (medico di base), specialist consultations, hospital stays, surgical procedures, and most diagnostic tests and medications. Many of these services are provided free of charge or for a small co-payment known as a "ticket." The ticket system is designed to prevent overuse of services and can vary by region and service type. For example, a visit to your primary care doctor is typically free, while you might pay a small fee for a specialist visit or diagnostic test.

One of the cornerstones of the Italian healthcare system is the role of the primary care doctor, or medico di base. This doctor serves as your first point of contact for most health issues and acts as a gatekeeper to specialist services. When you register with the SSN, you'll choose your primary care doctor from a list provided by your local ASL. It's worth taking some time to select a doctor who speaks English if your Italian isn't fluent, as this can greatly ease communication about health matters. Your primary care doctor can provide basic care, write prescriptions, and refer you to specialists when necessary.

Specialist care in Italy is generally of high quality, with many Italian hospitals and clinics equipped with advanced medical technology. However, one challenge you might face is waiting times for non-urgent procedures or specialist appointments. These can be quite long in the public system, sometimes extending to several months. This is one area where having additional private insurance can be beneficial, as it often allows you to bypass long waiting lists by accessing private clinics.

For retirees with chronic health conditions, Italy's approach to managing long-term illnesses is worth noting. The SSN provides comprehensive coverage for a range of chronic diseases, including diabetes, hypertension, and many forms of cancer. Patients with certified chronic conditions often receive priority in scheduling appointments and may be exempt from ticket payments for treatments related to their condition. This can be a significant benefit for retirees managing ongoing health issues.

Emergency care in Italy is provided through a network of emergency rooms (pronto soccorso) and the 118 emergency telephone service. Emergency care is provided to everyone, regardless of nationality or insurance status, although non-residents may be billed for services after treatment. It's important to note that emergency rooms in Italy use a triage system, with patients seen based on the severity of their condition rather than order of arrival. For non-emergency situations, there are also walk-in clinics (guardia medica) available for after-hours care.

While the public healthcare system in Italy is comprehensive, many expats and retirees choose to supplement their SSN coverage with private health insurance. There are several reasons for this. Private insurance can provide faster access to specialist care, more choice in healthcare providers, and coverage for services that might not be fully covered by the SSN, such as dental care or certain types of physiotherapy. Additionally, private insurance often offers more extensive coverage when traveling outside of Italy, which can be important for retirees who plan to travel frequently.

When considering private health insurance options in Italy, you'll find both local and international providers. Local Italian insurance companies may offer policies that are well-tailored to the Italian healthcare system but might have more limited coverage outside of Italy. International health insurance providers, on the other hand, often offer more comprehensive global coverage but may be more expensive. Some popular international providers for expats in Italy include Cigna Global, Allianz Care, and Bupa Global.

When choosing a private insurance plan, there are several factors to consider. First, check the geographical coverage – does the plan cover you just in Italy, throughout Europe, or worldwide? If you plan to travel frequently or spend part of the year in your home country, a plan with broader geographical coverage might be beneficial. Next, look at the specifics of what's covered. Does the plan include outpatient care, hospitalization, emergency evacuation, and repatriation? What about dental care, vision care, or alternative therapies? Also, pay attention to any waiting periods, especially for pre-existing conditions, and understand how the claims process works.

It's also worth noting that some Italian private insurance plans operate on a reimbursement basis, meaning you'll need to pay for services upfront and then submit a claim for reimbursement. This is different from systems in some other countries where the insurance company pays the healthcare provider directly. Make sure you're comfortable with the payment and reimbursement process of any plan you're considering.

For retirees from the United States, it's important to understand how Medicare interacts with healthcare in Italy. Medicare generally does not cover health services outside the United States, with a few rare exceptions. This means that if you're relying on Medicare, you'll need to arrange alternative coverage for your time in Italy. Some Medicare Advantage plans offer limited coverage for emergency care abroad, but this is typically for short trips rather than long-term residence. Therefore, it's crucial for American retirees to factor in the cost of either joining the SSN or purchasing comprehensive private health insurance when budgeting for retirement in Italy.

Prescription medications are another important consideration for many retirees. In Italy, medications are classified into three categories: Class A drugs are considered essential and are covered by the SSN with a small co-pay; Class C drugs are paid for entirely by the patient; and Class H drugs are only administered in hospitals. If you're taking regular medications, it's a good idea to research whether they're available in Italy and under what classification. In some cases, you might find that medications you're used to are not available in Italy, or they might be sold under different brand names. It's advisable to bring a supply of your medications with you when you first move, along with a letter from your doctor explaining your prescriptions.

Pharmacies (farmacie) play a significant role in the Italian healthcare system. They're easily identifiable by the green cross sign and are staffed by trained professionals who can offer advice on minor health issues and over-the-counter medications. Many common medications that might require a prescription in other countries are available over the counter in Italy. Pharmacies operate on a rotation system for night and holiday coverage, with information about the nearest open pharmacy posted on the door of any closed pharmacy.

For retirees with mobility issues or those who may need assistance as they age, it's worth understanding Italy's approach to long-term care. While the SSN provides some long-term care services, including home care and nursing home care, the system relies heavily on family support. This cultural expectation of family care can sometimes mean that formal long-term care services are less developed than in some other countries. However, there are options available, including public and private nursing homes (case di riposo) and home care services. These services can be expensive if not covered by the SSN, so it's something to consider in your long-term financial planning.

Mental health is an important aspect of overall well-being, particularly during a major life transition like retiring abroad. The SSN provides mental health services, including psychiatric care and psychotherapy, although waiting times can be long and finding an English-speaking therapist through the public system can be challenging. Many expats and retirees find that private insurance that covers mental health services, or budgeting for out-of-pocket therapy, is a worthwhile investment for their mental well-being.

Dental care is another area where the public and private systems in Italy differ significantly. The SSN provides only basic dental services, primarily for children and individuals with specific medical conditions. Most adults, including retirees, will need to pay out of pocket for dental care or have private insurance that covers dental services. The good news is that dental care in Italy is generally of high quality and can be more affordable than in countries like the United States.

For retirees who enjoy an active lifestyle, Italy offers excellent opportunities for maintaining physical health. The Mediterranean climate in much of the country encourages outdoor activities year-round. Many Italian cities are walkable, promoting daily physical activity as part of your routine. Additionally, many communities offer exercise classes or sports activities geared towards older adults. Participating in these can not only benefit your health but also help you integrate into your local community.

One aspect of healthcare that's particularly relevant for retirees is preventive care. The SSN places a strong emphasis on prevention, offering a range of screening programs for conditions like breast cancer, cervical cancer, and colorectal cancer. These screenings are typically free of charge for individuals in the relevant age groups. Taking advantage of these preventive services can help you maintain good health and catch any potential issues early.

As you settle into your life in Italy, you may find that your approach to health and wellness evolves. The Italian lifestyle, with its emphasis on fresh, seasonal foods, regular physical activity (even if it's just a daily passeggiata), and strong social connections, can contribute positively to your overall health. Many retirees find that they naturally adopt healthier habits as they embrace the Italian way of life.

Navigating a new healthcare system in a foreign language can be challenging, but there are resources available to help. Many hospitals and clinics in areas popular with expats have international patient offices that can provide assistance in English. There are also private patient advocacy services that can help you navigate the system, translate medical documents, and even accompany you to appointments if needed. While these services come at a cost, many retirees find them invaluable, especially when dealing with complex health issues.

It's also worth noting that Italy has a strong tradition of thermal spas and wellness centers, many of which are recognized by the SSN for their therapeutic benefits. Treatments at these centers can sometimes be prescribed by your doctor and partially covered by the national health service, particularly for conditions like arthritis or respiratory issues. Even if not medically necessary, many retirees find that regular visits to thermal spas contribute positively to their overall well-being.

As you prepare for your move to Italy, there are several health-related steps you can take to ensure a smooth transition. First, gather all your medical records and have them translated into Italian if possible. This will help your new Italian doctors understand your medical history. If you're taking any medications, research their availability in Italy and consider asking your current doctor for a supply to tide you over during the transition period. It's also a good idea to have a thorough check-up and any necessary dental work done before you move.

Once you're settled in Italy, take the time to familiarize yourself with the local healthcare resources. Learn the location of the nearest hospital, emergency room, and 24-hour pharmacy. If possible, schedule a get-to-know-you visit with your new primary care doctor, even if you're not sick. This can help establish a relationship and ensure that the doctor is aware of any ongoing health concerns you may have.

Remember that adjusting to a new healthcare system is a process, and it's normal to feel some anxiety or frustration at times. Be patient with yourself and don't hesitate to ask for help when you need it, whether from your local ASL, an patient advocate, or fellow expats who have gone through the same process.

In summary, while navigating the Italian healthcare system as a retiree may present some challenges, it also offers significant benefits. The combination of high-quality care, universal coverage, and the health-promoting aspects of the Italian lifestyle can contribute significantly to your well-being during your retirement years. By understanding your options, planning ahead, and embracing the local approach to health and wellness, you can look forward to a healthy and fulfilling retirement in Italy. Whether you're strolling through a picturesque piazza, savoring a leisurely meal with friends, or exploring the country's rich cultural heritage, you can do so with the peace of mind that comes from knowing you have access to excellent healthcare. Your health is a crucial part of enjoying la dolce vita, and Italy's healthcare system is there to support you every step of the way.

Chapter 6
Integrating into Italian Society

As you embark on your retirement journey in Italy, one of the most rewarding and challenging aspects will be integrating into Italian society. This process of immersion goes beyond simply living in Italy; it involves embracing the culture, customs, and daily rhythms of Italian life. Successfully integrating into Italian society can transform your retirement from a mere change of location to a rich, fulfilling experience that opens up new perspectives and ways of living. This chapter will guide you through the nuances of Italian culture, help you navigate potential language barriers, and provide strategies for building a vibrant social life in your new home.

The cornerstone of successful integration into any society is language, and Italy is no exception. While it's possible to get by in tourist areas with English, truly immersing yourself in Italian society requires at least a basic grasp of the Italian language. Learning Italian will not only make daily tasks easier but will also open doors to deeper connections with locals and a more authentic experience of Italian culture. The good news is that it's never too late to learn a new language, and many retirees find that the process of learning Italian keeps their minds sharp and provides a sense of accomplishment.

There are numerous ways to approach learning Italian. Many retirees find success with a combination of formal classes and informal practice. Before your move, consider starting with language learning apps like Duolingo or Babbel, which can help you grasp basic vocabulary and grammar. Once in Italy, look for language schools that offer courses specifically designed for adults or retirees. These classes often focus on practical, conversational Italian and can be an excellent way to meet other expats in similar situations.

Immersion is key to language learning, so don't be afraid to practice your Italian in daily life. Start with simple interactions like ordering coffee at a café or buying produce at a local market. Italians are generally patient and appreciative of foreigners attempting to speak their language, so don't worry about making mistakes. Each interaction is an opportunity to learn and improve. Consider joining language exchange groups where you can practice Italian with locals who want to improve their English. These exchanges can often lead to friendships and provide insights into local culture.

While mastering Italian takes time, even basic proficiency can greatly enhance your daily life and interactions. Learn key phrases for politeness (please, thank you, excuse me), as well as vocabulary related to your specific needs and interests. If you have health conditions, for example, learning medical terms in Italian can be very helpful. Remember that Italian is a language rich in gestures and body language, so pay attention to non-verbal communication as well.

As you work on overcoming the language barrier, you'll also encounter cultural differences that may take some adjustment. Italian culture is known for its warmth and emphasis on personal relationships, but it also has its own set of social norms and expectations that may differ from what you're accustomed to. Understanding and adapting to these cultural nuances is key to feeling at home in Italy.

One of the most noticeable aspects of Italian culture is the importance placed on family and personal relationships. Italians tend to have strong family ties, with extended families often playing a significant role in daily life. As a retiree, you may find that your neighbors take a keen interest in your life, offering help and including you in social gatherings. While this might feel intrusive at first if you're from a culture that values more personal space, embrace it as a genuine expression of welcome and care.

The Italian concept of time may also require some adjustment. Life in Italy often moves at a slower pace than in many other Western countries, particularly in smaller towns and rural areas. Shops may close for extended lunch breaks, and dinner is usually eaten later in the evening. Meetings and appointments may not always start exactly on time, and tasks might take longer to complete than you're used to. Rather than feeling frustrated by this, try to embrace the more relaxed approach to time. Many retirees find that this slower pace of life reduces stress and allows for a greater appreciation of day-to-day pleasures.

Food plays a central role in Italian culture, and mealtimes are often social events that can last for hours. Lunch is typically the main meal of the day, especially in smaller towns, and dinner is usually eaten later, around 8 or 9 pm. If you're invited to an Italian home for a meal, be prepared for multiple courses and don't be surprised if the host insists on serving you more food. Refusing food can be seen as impolite, so if you're full, it's better to accept a small portion and compliment the cook. Learning about local cuisine and food traditions can be a wonderful way to connect with your new community.

Dressing appropriately is another aspect of Italian culture to consider. Italians generally take pride in their appearance and tend to dress well, even for casual occasions. While you don't need to be fashionable all the time, making an effort to dress neatly, especially when going out in public, will help you blend in and show respect for local customs. This is particularly true when visiting churches or religious sites, where modest dress is expected.

Italian social etiquette might differ from what you're used to in subtle ways. For example, when meeting someone for the first time, a handshake is appropriate, but once you know someone better, greeting kisses on both cheeks are common (start with the left cheek). Using formal titles (Signore for men, Signora for women) is common until you're invited to use someone's first name. Being aware of these social norms can help you navigate social situations more comfortably.

As you settle into your new life in Italy, building a social network will be crucial for your happiness and well-being. While the language barrier might seem daunting at first, there are many ways to connect with both locals and fellow expats. One of the best ways to meet people is through shared interests and activities. Italy offers a wealth of opportunities for engagement, whether your interests lie in art, history, food, sports, or nature.

Consider joining local clubs or associations related to your hobbies. Many towns have groups for activities like hiking, book clubs, or amateur sports. These can be excellent ways to meet like-minded people and practice your Italian in a relaxed setting. If you're interested in Italian culture and history, look for cultural associations that organize talks, exhibitions, or excursions to local sites of interest. Participating in these activities not only helps you build connections but also deepens your understanding and appreciation of your new home.

Volunteering can be another rewarding way to integrate into your community and meet people. Many organizations in Italy welcome volunteers, from animal shelters to cultural heritage sites. Volunteering not only allows you to contribute to your new community but also provides opportunities to practice your language skills and meet both locals and fellow expats.

For those interested in continuing education, many Italian universities offer courses for older adults through programs often called "Università della Terza Età" (University of the Third Age). These programs provide a wide range of courses, from language and literature to art history and local traditions, often at very reasonable prices. Attending these classes can be an excellent way to keep your mind active, learn more about Italian culture, and meet other retirees with similar interests.

Religious institutions can also play a role in community integration, if that aligns with your beliefs. Even if you're not particularly religious, the local church often serves as a community hub in many Italian towns, organizing social events and charity initiatives that can provide opportunities for involvement.

While integrating with the local community should be a priority, connecting with other expats can also be valuable, especially in the early stages of your move. Other foreigners who have been in Italy longer can provide practical advice and support as you navigate your new life. Look for expat groups in your area – many organize regular meetups, language exchanges, or social events. Online platforms like InterNations or Meetup can be useful for finding these groups. However, try to strike a balance between expat and local connections to ensure a well-rounded social life and full immersion in Italian culture.

One of the joys of retiring in Italy is the opportunity to participate in local festivals and traditions. Nearly every town in Italy, no matter how small, has its own festivals or sagre (food festivals) celebrating local products, saints, or historical events. These events are not just for tourists; they're an integral part of community life and participating in them can help you feel more connected to your new home. Don't be shy about asking neighbors or local shopkeepers about upcoming events and how you can get involved.

The Italian tradition of the passeggiata, or evening stroll, is another simple yet effective way to integrate into community life. In many towns, particularly in the warmer months, locals gather in the main square or promenade in the early evening to walk, chat, and socialize. Joining in this daily ritual can help you become a familiar face in your community and provide opportunities for casual social interactions.

As you work on building your social network, be patient with yourself and the process. Integration takes time, and it's normal to experience periods of frustration or homesickness. Many retirees find that the first year is the most challenging as they adjust to new routines and cultural norms. Remember that it's okay to seek support when you need it, whether from new friends, expat groups, or professional services like counselors who specialize in helping foreigners adjust to life in Italy.

One aspect of Italian social life that may be new to you is the importance of your local bar or café. In Italy, the bar is not just a place to drink alcohol; it's a community hub where people gather for their morning coffee, a quick lunch, or an evening aperitivo. Becoming a regular at your local bar can be a great way to meet neighbors and feel part of the community. Don't be surprised if the barista starts preparing your usual order as soon as you walk in – this is a sign that you're becoming a familiar face.

Building relationships with local shopkeepers is another important aspect of integrating into Italian society. In many towns, people still shop at small, specialized stores rather than large supermarkets. Regular visits to your local baker, grocer, or butcher can lead to friendly relationships where you're not just a customer, but part of the community. These relationships can be invaluable, providing not just a sense of belonging but also access to local knowledge and sometimes even help with navigating bureaucratic processes.

As you become more comfortable in your new environment, consider hosting gatherings yourself. Inviting both expat friends and Italian neighbors for a meal or aperitivo can help bridge different social circles and deepen your connections. Don't worry if your Italian cooking skills aren't perfect – your guests will appreciate the effort and the opportunity to socialize.

Engaging with local politics and community issues can also help you feel more integrated. While as a foreigner you may not have voting rights in national elections, EU citizens can vote in local elections, and many towns allow resident foreigners to participate in local referendums or community councils. Even if you can't vote, staying informed about local issues and attending community meetings can help you feel more connected to your adopted home.

Learning about and respecting Italian business and bureaucratic customs is another important aspect of integration. Italians generally place a high value on personal relationships, even in business settings. This means that processes might take longer than you're used to, as time is spent building rapport. While this can be frustrating, especially when dealing with bureaucratic procedures, understanding and adapting to this cultural norm can make your interactions smoother and more pleasant.

Italy's rich artistic and cultural heritage offers countless opportunities for engagement and learning. Consider taking courses in traditional crafts, art history, or even Italian cooking. Many areas have local artisans who offer workshops in traditional skills like ceramics, leatherworking, or pasta making. Engaging in these activities not only provides a deeper appreciation of Italian culture but can also be a way to meet people and potentially discover new passions.

As you integrate into Italian society, you may find that your own perspectives and habits begin to change. Many retirees report that they become more relaxed, learn to enjoy life's simple pleasures more fully, and gain a new appreciation for quality over quantity in many aspects of life. Embrace these changes as part of your growth and adaptation to your new home.

One challenge you might face is maintaining connections with family and friends back home while building your new life in Italy. Modern technology makes this easier than ever, with video calls and social media allowing you to stay in touch despite the distance. However, it's important to strike a balance between maintaining these connections and fully engaging with your new life in Italy. Consider setting regular times for calls with family, but also make sure to stay present and engaged in your day-to-day life in Italy.

If you have grandchildren, think about ways to involve them in your new life. You might teach them a few words of Italian during video calls, share stories about your experiences, or even involve them in planning their future visits to see you. This can help maintain strong family bonds despite the geographical distance.

As you become more integrated into Italian society, you may find yourself becoming an informal ambassador for your home country. Italians are often curious about other cultures, and you may find yourself explaining customs or traditions from your home country. This cultural exchange can be enriching for both you and your new Italian friends.

Remember that integration is not about completely abandoning your own cultural identity, but rather about finding a harmonious balance between your background and your new Italian life. You bring unique perspectives and experiences to your new community, and these can be valuable contributions to cultural exchange and mutual understanding.

Lastly, be kind to yourself throughout this process. Integrating into a new society is a significant undertaking, and it's natural to have ups and downs. Celebrate your successes, whether it's successfully navigating a complicated conversation in Italian, being invited to a neighbor's family gathering, or simply feeling at home in your local café. Each small step is a victory on your journey to making Italy your home.

In summary, integrating into Italian society is a multifaceted process that involves language learning, cultural adaptation, and active community engagement. It requires patience, openness, and a willingness to step out of your comfort zone. However, the rewards are immeasurable. As you navigate this journey, you'll not only build a new life in one of the world's most beautiful countries, but you'll also likely discover new aspects of yourself. The friendships you form, the traditions you embrace, and the experiences you accumulate will all contribute to a rich and fulfilling retirement. Remember, the goal isn't to become Italian, but to find your own unique place within Italian society – a place where you can appreciate and contribute to the local culture while still honoring your own background and identity. As you immerse yourself in the rhythms of Italian life, from the morning espresso to the evening passeggiata, you'll find that Italy becomes not just the country where you retired, but truly your home.

Chapter 7
Everyday Life in Italy

As you settle into your retirement in Italy, you'll find that everyday life takes on a new rhythm, shaped by the unique blend of modern conveniences and age-old traditions that characterize this beautiful country. This chapter will guide you through the practicalities of daily living in Italy, from setting up utilities and navigating transportation to embracing local shopping habits and maintaining a healthy lifestyle. Understanding these aspects of everyday life will help you transition smoothly into your new home and fully appreciate the nuances of Italian living.

One of the first practical matters you'll need to address when setting up your new home in Italy is utilities. The process of activating utilities such as electricity, gas, and water can be somewhat different from what you're accustomed to, and may require a bit of patience. In Italy, you typically have the freedom to choose your electricity and gas providers, as the energy market is liberalized. This can be both an advantage and a challenge, as you'll need to research different providers to find the best rates and services for your needs. Water, on the other hand, is usually provided by a single municipal or regional company.

To set up your utilities, you'll need your codice fiscale (Italian tax code), a copy of your rental contract or property deed, and a valid form of identification. Many utility companies now offer the option to sign up online, which can be convenient, especially if you're not yet fluent in Italian. However, don't be surprised if you're asked to visit a local office to complete the process, particularly for water services. It's a good idea to ask your real estate agent or landlord for recommendations on reliable utility providers in your area.

When it comes to electricity, it's important to be aware of the concept of potenza impegnata, or contracted power level. This determines the maximum amount of electricity you can use simultaneously. The standard level for most apartments is 3 kW, but you may need to increase this if you have high-consumption appliances or a larger home. Adjusting your power level can affect your bills, so it's worth considering your electricity needs carefully.

Gas is used in many Italian homes for cooking and heating. If you're in an apartment building, you may have centralized heating (riscaldamento centralizzato), where the cost is shared among all residents. In other cases, you'll have an independent system and will need to contract directly with a gas provider. Be prepared for potentially high heating bills in the winter, especially if you're in an older, less insulated home.

Water bills in Italy typically come every three or four months and often include charges for sewage and waste disposal services. In some areas, you may need to provide meter readings to ensure accurate billing. It's also worth noting that tap water in Italy is generally safe to drink, although many Italians prefer bottled water for taste reasons.

Internet and phone services are another essential aspect of setting up your home. Italy has been making significant strides in improving its internet infrastructure, with fiber optic connections becoming increasingly available, especially in urban areas. However, connection speeds can still vary widely depending on your location. When choosing an internet provider, consider factors such as contract length, connection speed, and any bundled services like landline or mobile phone plans. Major providers in Italy include TIM, Vodafone, Wind, and Fastweb, among others. If you're in a more rural area, you might need to consider alternative solutions like satellite internet.

For mobile phone services, you have the option of prepaid plans (molto popolare in Italy) or contract plans. Prepaid plans can be a good option if you want more flexibility, while contract plans might offer better rates for heavy users. Remember that to get a mobile phone contract, you'll typically need to have a bank account in Italy. When choosing a plan, consider not just calls and texts within Italy, but also your needs for communicating with family and friends abroad. Many providers offer special international calling packages that can help keep costs down.

Transportation is another crucial aspect of daily life to consider. Italy has an extensive public transportation network, particularly in and between major cities. Trains are a popular and efficient way to travel between cities, with both high-speed (Alta Velocità) and regional services available. If you plan to use trains frequently, consider getting a Carta Argento, a discount card for seniors that offers significant savings on ticket prices.

Within cities and towns, buses are often the primary form of public transportation, supplemented by trams, metros, and light rail systems in larger cities. Many towns offer discounted or free public transportation passes for seniors, so be sure to inquire about these options. Taxis are readily available in cities but can be expensive, especially if called rather than hailed on the street. Ride-sharing services like Uber are available in some major cities, but their operations are more limited compared to many other countries.

If you're considering driving in Italy, be prepared for some adjustment. Italian driving can be more aggressive than what you might be used to, especially in larger cities. Narrow streets, limited parking, and zones of limited traffic (Zone a Traffico Limitato or ZTL) in many historic town centers can make driving challenging. However, having a car can be very convenient, especially if you're living in a rural area or plan to explore the countryside frequently. Remember that you'll need to obtain an Italian driver's license within a year of establishing residency, which may involve taking both written and practical tests unless your home country has a license conversion agreement with Italy.

For short trips around town, you might consider a bicycle or motorino (scooter). Many Italian towns are quite bicycle-friendly, and electric bikes are becoming increasingly popular, especially among retirees. Scooters can be a convenient way to navigate city traffic and find parking easily, but make sure you're comfortable with the idea of weaving through Italian traffic before committing to this option.

Shopping habits in Italy may differ from what you're accustomed to, particularly if you're coming from a country where large supermarkets dominate. While supermarkets certainly exist in Italy, many Italians still prefer to shop at small, specialized stores for many of their needs. This might include the fornaio (baker) for bread, the macellaio (butcher) for meat, the fruttivendolo (greengrocer) for fruits and vegetables, and the salumeria for cured meats and cheeses. Shopping this way not only often results in fresher, higher-quality products but also provides opportunities for social interaction and becoming part of the community.

Markets are another important part of Italian shopping culture. Most towns have a weekly outdoor market where you can find everything from fresh produce to clothing and household goods. These markets are not just places to shop but social events, where locals gather to chat and catch up on community news. Embracing this style of shopping can be a wonderful way to immerse yourself in local life and practice your Italian.

When it comes to groceries, you'll find that the emphasis on seasonal, local produce in Italy means that the availability of certain fruits and vegetables changes throughout the year. This can be an adjustment if you're used to having all produce available year-round, but it also means that you'll be eating fresher, more flavorful foods. Many retirees find that they naturally adopt a healthier diet in Italy simply by following local eating habits.

For non-food items, you'll find a mix of small, independent shops and larger chain stores. Department stores (grandi magazzini) like Coin or La Rinascente offer a wide range of products under one roof. For home goods and DIY supplies, stores like Leroy Merlin or Bricofer are similar to home improvement stores you might be familiar with. Online shopping is also becoming increasingly popular in Italy, with both international platforms like Amazon and local e-commerce sites available.

One aspect of shopping in Italy that might take some getting used to is the more limited store hours compared to some countries. Many shops close for a long lunch break (typically from around 1:00 PM to 3:30 or 4:00 PM) and are closed on Sundays, although this is changing in larger cities and tourist areas. It's also worth noting that many small businesses close for several weeks in August for the traditional summer holiday. Planning your shopping around these hours becomes second nature over time, and many retirees find that they come to appreciate the slower pace and emphasis on work-life balance that these customs reflect.

Dining is, of course, one of the great pleasures of life in Italy. While cooking at home with fresh, local ingredients can be a joy, eating out is an important part of Italian social life. Understanding the structure of Italian meals and dining customs can enhance your experience. A typical Italian meal consists of an antipasto (appetizer), primo (first course, usually pasta or rice), secondo (main course, typically meat or fish) with contorno (side dish), followed by dolce (dessert). However, it's perfectly acceptable to order just a primo or secondo if you don't want a full meal.

Breakfast in Italy is typically a light affair, often just a coffee and a sweet pastry, often consumed standing at the bar of a café. Lunch was traditionally the main meal of the day, though this is changing in bigger cities. Dinner is usually eaten later than in many other countries, with restaurants often not opening until 7:30 or 8:00 PM. The evening meal is often a social event, lingering over multiple courses and conversation.

When dining out, be aware of coperto, a per-person cover charge that is standard in many restaurants. This usually includes bread and should be listed on the menu. Tipping is not as expected in Italy as it is in some countries; if you're pleased with the service, rounding up the bill or leaving a small amount is appreciated but not required.

Italy's café culture is an integral part of daily life. The local bar (which is more akin to a café than a pub) is a social hub where people gather for their morning coffee, a quick lunch, or an evening aperitivo. Learning to order and enjoy your coffee like a local – standing at the bar, drinking your espresso quickly – can be a small but satisfying way of integrating into Italian daily life.

Maintaining a healthy lifestyle in Italy can feel quite natural, as many aspects of Italian culture promote well-being. The Mediterranean diet, rich in fresh vegetables, fruits, whole grains, and healthy fats like olive oil, is renowned for its health benefits. Many retirees find that they naturally adopt healthier eating habits simply by embracing local food customs.

Physical activity is often built into daily life in Italy, especially if you're living in a walkable town or city. The tradition of the passeggiata, or evening stroll, is not just a social custom but a gentle form of daily exercise. Many towns have beautiful parks or seafront promenades that are perfect for walking or jogging. Cycling is popular in many areas, and you'll find that many towns have bike paths or bike-sharing programs.

If you prefer more structured exercise, you'll find gyms (palestre) in most towns, often offering classes tailored for older adults. Swimming is another popular form of exercise, with many towns having public pools or beach clubs. In coastal areas, swimming in the sea is a beloved activity during the warmer months.

Italy's abundant natural beauty also offers countless opportunities for outdoor activities. Depending on where you live, you might have access to hiking trails, ski resorts, golf courses, or water sports. Joining a local club dedicated to your favorite outdoor activity can be a great way to stay active and meet people.

Mental well-being is also an important aspect of a healthy lifestyle, and many retirees find that life in Italy naturally promotes a sense of balance and reduces stress. The emphasis on taking time to enjoy meals, the importance placed on social connections, and the general appreciation for life's pleasures all contribute to a sense of well-being. Many towns offer courses or groups dedicated to activities like painting, music, or language learning, which can provide mental stimulation and social connections.

Managing healthcare in your daily life is another important consideration. As discussed in a previous chapter, you'll have access to Italy's national healthcare system once you're a resident. For routine care, you'll typically start with your medico di base (general practitioner). It's a good idea to locate the nearest pharmacy (farmacia) to your home, identifiable by a green cross sign. Pharmacists in Italy are highly trained and can offer advice on minor health issues and over-the-counter medications.

Dealing with bureaucracy is an inevitable part of life in Italy, and it's an aspect that many foreigners find challenging at first. Patience is key when dealing with Italian bureaucracy, as processes can often take longer than you might expect. It's not uncommon for officials to interpret rules differently, so you might get varying answers to the same question. When dealing with any official matters, it's always a good idea to bring multiple photocopies of any required documents, as well as your passport and permesso di soggiorno.

One practical tip for navigating daily life in Italy is to always carry some cash with you. While card payments are becoming more common, there are still many small businesses, especially in smaller towns, that prefer or only accept cash. On the other hand, for larger purchases or bill payments, many Italians use bank transfers rather than checks, which are less common in Italy.

Adapting to the rhythm of Italian life is part of the joy of retiring in Italy. You'll likely find that life moves at a slower pace, especially outside of the major cities. Shops and offices may close for extended lunch breaks, and the month of August sees many businesses close entirely for summer holidays. Rather than finding this frustrating, try to embrace this lifestyle. Use the quieter afternoon hours for a siesta, catching up on reading, or enjoying a leisurely lunch with friends.

The changing seasons play a significant role in Italian life, affecting everything from what's available in the markets to local festivals and activities. Each season brings its own pleasures: spring with its fresh vegetables and Easter celebrations, summer with its long evenings perfect for outdoor dining, autumn with its harvest festivals and new wine, and winter with its hearty cuisine and holiday traditions. Learning to live in harmony with these seasonal rhythms can greatly enhance your enjoyment of life in Italy.

Technology can be both a help and a hindrance in daily life. While Italy has been making strides in digital services, you may find that some aspects of life are less digitized than what you're used to. However, smartphones can be incredibly useful for everything from navigating public transportation to translating menus. Many cities have apps that provide information on local services, events, and transportation. It's also worth noting that Italy has strict privacy laws, so you may need to provide explicit consent for various data uses more frequently than in some other countries.

Understanding and adapting to local customs around noise can be important for harmonious living, especially if you're in an apartment. Italians generally observe quiet hours (usually 1:00 PM to 3:00 PM and 10:00 PM to 8:00 AM), during which excessive noise should be avoided. On the other hand, you may need to accustom yourself to the sounds of daily Italian life, from animated conversations in the street to the ringing of church bells.

Waste management is taken seriously in Italy, with extensive recycling programs in most areas. You'll likely need to separate your waste into different categories (e.g., organic, paper, plastic, glass, and non-recyclable), and there may be specific days for collection of each type. While it might seem complex at first, most retirees find that they quickly adapt to these eco-friendly practices.

One of the joys of daily life in Italy is the abundance of cultural events and activities available, often at low or no cost. Many towns have regular concert series, art exhibitions, or film screenings. During the summer months, it's common for towns to host outdoor film screenings or concerts in main squares or parks. Keep an eye out for posters around town or check local news websites to stay informed about these events.

Religious traditions still play a significant role in Italian cultural life, even for those who aren't particularly religious. Religious festivals often involve the whole community and can be fascinating cultural experiences. Even if you don't share the religious beliefs, participating in or observing these events can provide insight into local culture and history.

Building and maintaining social connections is a crucial part of daily life in Italy. Italians place great importance on personal relationships, and you'll likely find that socializing plays a larger role in your daily life than it might have in your home country. This might involve chatting with neighbors, having coffee with friends, or participating in community events. Embracing this aspect of Italian culture can greatly enrich your retirement experience.

As you settle into your new life, you may find yourself adopting new daily rituals that reflect the Italian way of life. This might be a morning espresso at your local bar, an afternoon passeggiata through town, or a weekly visit to the market. These small habits can help you feel more connected to your new home and community.

Retiring to Italy

Remember that adapting to daily life in a new country is a process, and it's normal to have moments of frustration or homesickness. Be patient with yourself as you navigate this new way of life. Many retirees find that keeping a journal of their experiences, both the challenges and the joys, can be a rewarding way to track their progress and appreciate their journey.

Everyday life in Italy as a retiree offers a unique blend of challenges and rewards. From navigating practical matters like utilities and transportation to embracing the pleasures of Italian food, culture, and social life, each day presents opportunities for new experiences and personal growth. By approaching these aspects of daily life with curiosity, patience, and openness, you can create a rich and fulfilling retirement lifestyle. The key is to find a balance between maintaining elements of your familiar lifestyle and embracing new Italian ways. As you become more comfortable with the rhythms of Italian life, you'll likely find that the initial challenges give way to a deep appreciation for the quality of life that Italy offers. Whether you're savoring a perfectly crafted cappuccino at your local bar, chatting with neighbors in the piazza, or simply enjoying the view from your terrace, you'll find that everyday life in Italy offers countless small pleasures that add up to a deeply satisfying retirement experience.

One aspect of daily life that many retirees come to appreciate is the Italian approach to time. While it can initially be frustrating if you're used to a more fast-paced lifestyle, many find that they come to value the slower, more deliberate pace of Italian life. This doesn't mean that things don't get done, but rather that there's a different priority placed on how time is spent. You may find yourself lingering over meals, taking time to chat with shopkeepers, or spending an afternoon people-watching in a café. This shift in perspective can lead to a more relaxed and enjoyable daily life.

The rhythm of the Italian day may also require some adjustment. Many businesses, especially in smaller towns, still observe the traditional riposo or pausa, closing for a few hours in the afternoon. While this can be inconvenient if you need to run errands, it also encourages a break in the day that many retirees come to appreciate. You might use this time for a leisurely lunch, a nap, or pursuing a hobby. As you adapt to this rhythm, you may find that it contributes to a more balanced and less stressful lifestyle.

Weather plays a significant role in daily life in Italy, influencing everything from what you wear to how you spend your time. Summers can be quite hot, especially in the south, leading many Italians to adjust their schedules to avoid the hottest part of the day. You might find yourself adopting habits like early morning walks or evening outings to enjoy cooler temperatures. Winters, while generally milder than in many parts of Northern Europe or North America, can still be chilly, especially in homes that may not have central heating. Learning to dress in layers and perhaps investing in a good space heater can help you stay comfortable.

One of the great joys of daily life in Italy is the opportunity to continually discover new aspects of your adopted home. Even after years of living in a place, you might stumble upon a hidden courtyard, a tiny trattoria serving spectacular food, or a breathtaking view you've never noticed before. Cultivating a sense of curiosity and openness can turn every outing into a potential adventure.

Managing finances in daily life may require some adjustment. While credit and debit cards are widely accepted, especially in larger towns and cities, cash is still king in many situations. You'll likely find yourself carrying more cash than you're used to, particularly for small purchases or in rural areas. It's also worth noting that many bills, such as utilities or property taxes, are typically paid through bank transfers rather than checks or online payments.

Staying connected with friends and family back home will likely be an important part of your daily life. Thanks to technology, this is easier than ever. Video calls, social media, and messaging apps can help you maintain close relationships despite the distance. However, it's important to strike a balance between staying in touch with your old life and fully engaging with your new one. Setting aside specific times for calls home can help you manage this balance.

Health and wellness may take on new dimensions in your daily life in Italy. The Mediterranean lifestyle, with its emphasis on fresh, seasonal food, regular physical activity, and strong social connections, can contribute significantly to your overall well-being. You might find yourself naturally adopting healthier habits, such as walking more, eating a diet rich in fruits and vegetables, and taking time to relax and de-stress.

Engaging with the local community can become a rewarding part of your daily routine. This might involve volunteering with a local organization, participating in community events, or simply becoming a regular at local businesses. As you become a familiar face in your community, you'll likely find that your daily interactions become richer and more meaningful.

Language learning will likely be an ongoing part of your daily life, even if you arrived in Italy with a good grasp of the language. You'll constantly be exposed to new vocabulary, idiomatic expressions, and regional dialects. Embracing this as a lifelong learning opportunity can be both challenging and rewarding. Don't be afraid to make mistakes – most Italians appreciate the effort and are happy to help you improve.

As you settle into your new life, you may find yourself reevaluating your priorities and what truly brings you joy. Many retirees report that living in Italy has led them to place greater value on experiences rather than material possessions, on relationships rather than achievements, and on quality of life rather than quantity of activities. This shift in perspective can be one of the most profound and rewarding aspects of retiring in Italy.

Remember that creating a satisfying daily life in Italy is a process, not a destination. There will be challenges and frustrations along the way, but also moments of pure joy and deep satisfaction. Embrace both as part of the rich tapestry of your retirement experience. Be patient with yourself as you navigate this new way of life, and don't hesitate to ask for help when you need it, whether from fellow expats, local friends, or professional services.

In the end, daily life in Italy as a retiree is what you make of it. It offers a unique blend of rich cultural experiences, beautiful surroundings, delicious food and wine, and a lifestyle that prioritizes enjoyment and connection. By approaching each day with curiosity, openness, and a willingness to embrace new experiences, you can create a retirement lifestyle that is truly fulfilling.

Whether you're sipping an espresso at your local bar, haggling over fresh produce at the market, enjoying a leisurely multi-course Sunday lunch with friends, or simply watching the sunset from your terrace, you'll find that everyday life in Italy offers countless opportunities for joy, growth, and connection. As you integrate these uniquely Italian experiences into your daily routine, you'll likely find that you're not just living in Italy, but truly living the Italian way of life.

This journey of adapting to and embracing everyday life in Italy is ongoing. Each day brings new opportunities to deepen your connection to your adopted home, to challenge yourself, to learn, and to grow. And as you navigate the complexities and joys of Italian daily life, you may find that you're not just creating a new lifestyle, but reinventing yourself in subtle yet profound ways.

In essence, retiring to Italy is not just about changing your location, but about embracing a new way of living. It's about savoring life's simple pleasures, valuing personal connections, and finding beauty in the everyday. As you continue to navigate and embrace the nuances of everyday life in Italy, you're not just retiring – you're embarking on a new adventure, one delicious meal, one breathtaking view, one warm conversation at a time.

Chapter 8
Leisure and Recreation

R etiring in Italy offers a unique opportunity to immerse yourself in a rich tapestry of leisure and recreational activities that cater to a wide range of interests and passions. From exploring the country's unparalleled cultural heritage to engaging in popular local pastimes, your retirement years in Italy promise to be filled with enriching experiences and joyful discoveries. In this chapter, we'll delve into the myriad ways you can spend your leisure time, exploring Italy's cultural treasures, embracing outdoor activities, and participating in local traditions that will make your retirement truly memorable.

One of the most rewarding aspects of retiring in Italy is the opportunity to explore the country's vast cultural heritage at your own pace. Italy is home to more UNESCO World Heritage sites than any other country in the world, boasting an astonishing array of historical and artistic treasures. From ancient Roman ruins to Renaissance masterpieces, every corner of Italy offers something to captivate and inspire. As a retiree, you have the luxury of time to truly appreciate these wonders, without the rush that often accompanies shorter visits.

Museums in Italy are not just repositories of art and artifacts; they are gateways to understanding the rich history and culture of the country. Major cities like Rome, Florence, and Venice are home to world-renowned museums that house some of the most important works of art in human history. The Vatican Museums in Rome, for instance, offer an awe-inspiring journey through centuries of art, culminating in the breathtaking Sistine Chapel. In Florence, the Uffizi Gallery showcases the finest collection of Italian Renaissance art in the world, while the Accademia Gallery is home to Michelangelo's iconic David. Venice's Peggy Guggenheim Collection, on the other hand, offers a more modern perspective with its impressive array of 20th-century art.

But it's not just the famous museums that deserve your attention. Smaller, lesser-known museums often provide equally enriching experiences. Many towns and even small villages have their own local museums that offer intimate glimpses into regional history, traditions, and artistic styles. These smaller institutions often have the advantage of being less crowded, allowing for a more personal and reflective experience.

For art enthusiasts, Italy offers countless opportunities to deepen your appreciation and understanding of various artistic movements and techniques. Many museums and cultural institutions offer guided tours, lectures, and workshops designed specifically for adults and seniors. These programs can provide valuable insights into the artworks and their historical context, enhancing your appreciation of what you're seeing. Some institutions even offer hands-on workshops where you can try your hand at traditional artistic techniques, from fresco painting to mosaic making.

Italy's historical sites are another treasure trove waiting to be explored. The country's long and complex history has left an indelible mark on its landscape, with remnants of ancient civilizations, medieval towns, and Renaissance palaces scattered throughout the country. In Rome, you can walk in the footsteps of ancient Romans at the Colosseum and Forum, or explore the winding streets of the medieval Trastevere neighborhood. In Pompeii and Herculaneum, near Naples, you can step back in time to the first century AD, wandering through remarkably preserved Roman towns frozen in time by the eruption of Mount Vesuvius.

Medieval hill towns in Tuscany and Umbria offer their own charms, with their narrow cobblestone streets, imposing fortresses, and picturesque piazzas. Places like Siena, San Gimignano, and Assisi not only offer stunning architecture but also provide a glimpse into the rich traditions and slower pace of life in these historic centers. Many of these towns host seasonal festivals and events that bring their history to life, offering unique opportunities to participate in local traditions.

For those interested in more recent history, Italy's numerous palaces and villas provide fascinating insights into the lives of the nobility and wealthy merchants who shaped the country's Renaissance and Baroque periods. The opulent Royal Palace of Caserta near Naples, the elegant Borghese Gallery and Gardens in Rome, and the stunning Palladian villas of the Veneto region are just a few examples of the architectural and artistic splendors awaiting exploration.

Theaters and opera houses represent another important facet of Italy's cultural landscape. Italy is the birthplace of opera, and attending a performance in one of the country's historic opera houses is an unforgettable experience. The Teatro alla Scala in Milan, the Teatro La Fenice in Venice, and the Teatro di San Carlo in Naples are among the most famous, but even smaller cities often have beautiful theaters with regular performances of opera, classical music, and drama. Many of these venues offer guided tours during the day, allowing you to appreciate their architectural beauty and learn about their rich histories.

For cinema enthusiasts, Italy offers a wealth of opportunities to explore both classic and contemporary Italian films. Many cities host film festivals throughout the year, showcasing Italian and international cinema. The Venice Film Festival, held annually on the Lido di Venezia, is one of the most prestigious in the world and offers a unique opportunity to see premiere screenings and possibly spot some celebrities. Smaller, themed film festivals in various towns provide more intimate settings to discover new films and meet fellow cinephiles.

Beyond the realms of art and history, Italy offers a wide array of outdoor activities and sports that cater to various interests and fitness levels. The country's diverse geography, from the Alpine peaks in the north to the sun-drenched coasts of the south, provides a natural playground for outdoor enthusiasts.

Hiking is a popular activity among retirees in Italy, offering a perfect blend of physical exercise and scenic beauty. The country boasts an extensive network of well-marked trails suitable for all levels of fitness and experience. In the north, the Dolomites offer breathtaking mountain scenery and a range of trails from easy walks to challenging climbs. The Cinque Terre, a string of five picturesque villages along the Ligurian coast, is famous for its coastal hiking trails that offer stunning sea views. In central Italy, the rolling hills of Tuscany and Umbria provide gentle, scenic walks often leading to charming hilltop towns or hidden monasteries.

For those who prefer two wheels, cycling is an excellent way to explore the Italian countryside. Many regions have developed extensive networks of cycling paths, often utilizing converted railway lines or quiet country roads. The Po River Delta in the Veneto region, for instance, offers flat, easy rides through a unique wetland ecosystem. In Tuscany, you can pedal through the iconic landscapes of the Val d'Orcia or the Chianti wine region. Many tour operators offer guided cycling tours tailored for seniors, complete with electric bike options for those who want a little extra assistance.

Water activities are another popular pastime, especially during the warm summer months. Italy's extensive coastline and numerous lakes offer ample opportunities for swimming, sailing, and other water sports. The Italian Riviera, the Amalfi Coast, and the islands of Sicily and Sardinia are renowned for their beautiful beaches and clear waters. Lake Como, Lake Garda, and Lake Maggiore in the north are popular destinations for sailing and windsurfing, with many local clubs offering courses and rentals.

For those who enjoy winter sports, the Italian Alps and Dolomites offer world-class skiing and snowboarding. Resorts like Cortina d'Ampezzo, Courmayeur, and Madonna di Campiglio cater to all levels of expertise and often have special programs and facilities for senior skiers. Even if you're not hitting the slopes, these mountain resorts offer beautiful winter scenery and cozy alpine atmospheres perfect for relaxation.

Golf is gaining popularity in Italy, with numerous courses scattered throughout the country. Many of these courses are set in stunning locations, from seaside links to courses nestled in the Tuscan countryside. The mild climate in many parts of Italy allows for year-round golfing, making it an attractive option for retirees looking to improve their game.

One of the joys of retiring in Italy is the opportunity to immerse yourself in local traditions and pastimes. Each region, and often each town, has its own unique customs and activities that reflect its history and culture. Participating in these can be a wonderful way to integrate into your local community and experience authentic Italian life.

In many parts of Italy, particularly in smaller towns and rural areas, the local piazza remains the heart of community life. Spending time in these public squares, whether sipping a coffee at a café or simply people-watching from a bench, is a cherished pastime. It's a great way to observe local life, practice your Italian, and perhaps strike up conversations with neighbors.

Card games are a popular pastime among Italians of all ages, but particularly among retirees. Games like Scopa and Briscola are often played in local bars or social clubs, and joining in can be a great way to socialize and improve your language skills. Many towns have clubs or associations dedicated to various card games and board games, which welcome new members.

For those interested in more active pursuits, bocce (similar to boules or pétanque) is a traditional Italian game that's easy to learn and enjoy. Many parks and social clubs have bocce courts, and the game is a popular way for retirees to socialize and enjoy some gentle exercise.

Cooking classes and food tours have become increasingly popular among both locals and expatriates in Italy. Given the country's renowned culinary traditions, these activities offer a delightful way to deepen your appreciation of Italian cuisine and culture. Many cooking schools offer courses specifically designed for foreigners, teaching traditional recipes and techniques. These classes can range from short, single-day experiences to more comprehensive programs spanning several weeks or months.

Similarly, food and wine tours provide opportunities to explore Italy's gastronomic landscape. Whether it's visiting local markets with a knowledgeable guide, touring vineyards and olive groves, or sampling regional specialties in traditional trattorias, these experiences offer insights into the deep connection between food, land, and culture in Italy.

Gardening is another popular pastime among retirees in Italy, particularly for those who have relocated to rural areas or small towns. Many Italians take great pride in their vegetable gardens, growing fresh produce for their own consumption. Even in urban areas, balcony gardening and community garden projects are gaining popularity. Joining a local gardening club or community garden can be a wonderful way to learn about local plants and growing techniques while also socializing with like-minded individuals.

For those with a creative bent, Italy offers numerous opportunities to explore various crafts and artistic pursuits. Many towns have artisans practicing traditional crafts such as ceramics, glassblowing, leather working, and textiles. Taking classes or workshops in these traditional crafts can be a rewarding way to engage with local culture and perhaps discover a new hobby. Painting and photography are also popular pursuits, given Italy's inspiring landscapes and architectural beauty.

Volunteering is another fulfilling way to spend your leisure time in retirement. Many organizations in Italy welcome volunteers, particularly those with language skills who can assist with tourism, cultural events, or support services for other expatriates. Environmental organizations often seek volunteers for conservation projects, while many cultural institutions rely on volunteers to support their operations. Volunteering can be an excellent way to give back to your adopted community while also expanding your social network and gaining new skills.

Italy's calendar is filled with festivals and events throughout the year, many of which have roots in ancient traditions or religious observances. Participating in these events can offer unique insights into local culture and provide opportunities for celebration and community engagement. From the colorful Carnevale celebrations in Venice and Viareggio to the Palio horse race in Siena, these events showcase Italy's rich cultural heritage and zest for life.

Music festivals are another highlight of Italy's cultural calendar. The country hosts numerous festivals covering a wide range of musical genres. The Ravello Festival on the Amalfi Coast and the Spoleto Festival in Umbria are renowned for their classical music programs, often featuring performances in stunning outdoor settings. For jazz enthusiasts, the Umbria Jazz Festival in Perugia and the Roma Jazz Festival offer world-class performances in historic venues.

Literature lovers will find plenty to engage with in Italy. Many towns host literary festivals and book fairs throughout the year. The Festivaletteratura in Mantua, for instance, is one of Europe's leading literary events, attracting authors and readers from around the world. These events often include readings, discussions, and workshops, providing opportunities to engage with both Italian and international literature.

For those interested in lifelong learning, many universities and cultural institutions in Italy offer courses and lecture series designed for adults and retirees. These programs, often called "Università della Terza Età" (University of the Third Age), cover a wide range of subjects from art history and literature to science and current affairs. They provide excellent opportunities for intellectual stimulation and social interaction.

Language learning is another popular pursuit among retirees in Italy. While many Italians in tourist areas speak English, learning Italian can greatly enhance your experience of living in the country. It allows for deeper engagement with local culture and community life. Many language schools offer courses tailored for seniors, with flexible schedules and teaching methods adapted to adult learners. Joining a language exchange group, where you can practice Italian with locals who want to improve their English, can be a fun and social way to improve your language skills.

As you explore these various leisure and recreational activities, it's important to pace yourself and listen to your body. While retirement offers the freedom to pursue new interests and adventures, it's also a time to prioritize your health and well-being. Many of the activities mentioned can be adapted to different fitness levels and abilities, so don't hesitate to ask for accommodations or seek out senior-friendly options.

Remember also that leisure time in Italy is often about quality rather than quantity. The Italian concept of "dolce far niente" – the sweetness of doing nothing – is an art in itself. Sometimes, the most enjoyable moments can be found in simply sitting at a café, watching the world go by, or taking a leisurely stroll through a beautiful piazza.

As you settle into your retirement in Italy, you'll likely find that your leisure time takes on new dimensions. Activities that might have seemed like tourist experiences during shorter visits can become meaningful parts of your daily or weekly routine. You might find yourself becoming a regular at local cultural events, developing deep friendships through shared interests, or even rediscovering passions that you didn't have time to pursue during your working years.

Retiring to Italy

The key to enjoying leisure and recreation in your Italian retirement is to remain open to new experiences while also honoring your own interests and rhythms. Italy offers a wealth of opportunities to engage with art, history, nature, and local traditions, but it also respects the individual's right to relax and enjoy life at their own pace. Whether you choose to fill your days with cultural explorations, outdoor adventures, or quiet contemplation, you'll find that Italy provides the perfect backdrop for a rich and fulfilling retirement.

As you embark on this new chapter of your life, remember that leisure and recreation are not just about filling time, but about enriching your life, fostering new connections, and continuing to grow and learn. Embrace the opportunities that come your way, but also don't be afraid to create your own path. Your retirement in Italy is a unique journey, and how you choose to spend your leisure time will play a significant role in shaping this exciting new phase of your life.

Chapter 9
Navigating Italian Bureaucracy

As you embark on your retirement journey in Italy, one of the most challenging aspects you'll encounter is navigating the country's notorious bureaucracy. While Italy's rich culture, stunning landscapes, and delicious cuisine are often the focus of retirement dreams, the reality of dealing with administrative processes can sometimes feel like a rude awakening. However, with patience, preparation, and the right approach, you can successfully navigate these bureaucratic waters and fully enjoy your Italian retirement. In this chapter, we'll explore the intricacies of Italian bureaucracy, providing you with insights, strategies, and practical advice to help you manage everything from residency permits to driving licenses.

The first thing to understand about Italian bureaucracy is that it's deeply rooted in the country's history and culture. Italy as a unified nation is relatively young, having been formed only in 1861. Prior to unification, the Italian peninsula was divided into numerous independent states, each with its own systems and traditions. This historical context has contributed to a complex bureaucratic system that can sometimes seem labyrinthine to outsiders. However, it's important to remember that while the system may seem frustrating at times, it's designed to ensure fairness and adherence to the law.

One of the first bureaucratic hurdles you'll face when retiring in Italy is obtaining your residency permit, or "permesso di soggiorno." This document is crucial as it allows you to legally reside in Italy for an extended period. The process of obtaining a residency permit begins even before you arrive in Italy. You'll need to apply for a long-stay visa at the Italian embassy or consulate in your home country. Once you arrive in Italy, you have eight days to apply for your residency permit at the local Questura (police headquarters) or, in some cases, at the post office.

The application process for a residency permit can be complex and time-consuming. You'll need to fill out several forms, provide numerous documents (including proof of income, health insurance, and accommodation), and possibly attend an interview. It's crucial to ensure that all your documents are in order before submitting your application. Any missing or incorrect information can lead to delays or rejection of your application. Many retirees find it helpful to work with a local lawyer or immigration consultant who is familiar with the process and can guide you through it.

Once you've submitted your application, you'll receive a receipt which serves as a temporary residency document. Processing times for residency permits can vary greatly, from a few weeks to several months, depending on the workload of the local authorities. During this waiting period, it's important to keep this receipt with you at all times, as it serves as proof that you're legally in the country.

After you receive your residency permit, you'll need to register with the local Anagrafe (registry office) to obtain your certificato di residenza (certificate of residency). This document is essential for many aspects of daily life in Italy, from opening a bank account to accessing healthcare services. The process involves providing proof of your address in Italy, which could be a rental contract or a property deed if you've purchased a home.

One of the most important documents you'll need in Italy is the Codice Fiscale, which is similar to a social security number in other countries. This alphanumeric code is used for a wide range of activities, from paying taxes to signing up for utilities. You can obtain your Codice Fiscale at the local Agenzia delle Entrate (Italian Revenue Agency) office. The process is usually straightforward and can often be completed on the same day.

Healthcare is another area where you'll encounter Italian bureaucracy. If you're a citizen of an EU country, you can use your European Health Insurance Card (EHIC) for temporary stays. However, as a retiree planning to live in Italy long-term, you'll need to register with the Italian National Health Service (Servizio Sanitario Nazionale or SSN). This process involves presenting your residency permit, Codice Fiscale, and proof of income at your local ASL (Azienda Sanitaria Locale) office. Once registered, you'll receive a health card (tessera sanitaria) which gives you access to healthcare services in Italy.

For non-EU retirees, the process can be more complex. You may need to show proof of private health insurance that covers your entire stay in Italy when applying for your residency permit. It's crucial to ensure that your insurance policy meets the requirements set by Italian authorities. Some non-EU retirees choose to maintain private health insurance even after becoming eligible for the SSN, as it can provide additional coverage and potentially shorter wait times for certain procedures.

Dealing with taxes is another area where you'll encounter Italian bureaucracy. Italy has tax treaties with many countries to avoid double taxation, but you'll still need to declare your worldwide income to Italian tax authorities. The Italian tax system can be complex, with different rates and deductions applying to various types of income. Many retirees find it essential to work with a commercialista (accountant) who specializes in international tax issues to ensure they're complying with all relevant laws and regulations.

If you plan to drive in Italy, you'll need to navigate the process of obtaining an Italian driving license. For EU citizens, this process is relatively straightforward – you can simply exchange your EU license for an Italian one. However, for non-EU citizens, the process is more complex. Depending on your country of origin, you may need to take both a theory test and a practical driving test to obtain an Italian license. These tests are conducted in Italian, so language proficiency is crucial. Many retirees choose to enroll in a local driving school (scuola guida) to prepare for these tests and navigate the bureaucratic process of obtaining a license.

Another important aspect of Italian bureaucracy that retirees often encounter is related to property ownership. If you decide to purchase property in Italy, you'll need to navigate a complex system involving notaries, local authorities, and various regulations. The process of buying property in Italy typically involves several steps, including signing a preliminary contract (compromesso), obtaining necessary certifications, and finally signing the deed of sale (atto di vendita) in the presence of a notary. Each of these steps involves its own set of bureaucratic procedures and documentation requirements.

Even after purchasing a property, you'll need to deal with ongoing bureaucratic requirements. These include registering for and paying property taxes, obtaining certifications for various aspects of your property (such as energy efficiency), and complying with local regulations regarding property maintenance and renovations. If you're planning any significant renovations or changes to your property, you'll likely need to obtain permits from local authorities, a process that can be time-consuming and complex.

One aspect of Italian bureaucracy that often surprises retirees is the importance of official stamps and certifications. Many official documents in Italy require a "marca da bollo," a type of tax stamp that you can purchase at tobacco shops or post offices. These stamps are used to validate various documents and applications. Similarly, many official documents need to be authenticated or certified in specific ways. For example, you might need an "apostille" (a form of authentication recognized internationally) on certain documents from your home country before they can be used in Italy.

Navigating the Italian postal system can also be an adventure in bureaucracy. While the system has modernized in recent years, you may still encounter situations where you need to use registered mail (raccomandata) for official communications. This process involves filling out specific forms and keeping receipts as proof of mailing. Many official deadlines in Italy are based on the date of mailing (as proven by the postmark) rather than the date of receipt, so understanding how to use the postal system correctly can be crucial.

One strategy that many retirees find helpful when dealing with Italian bureaucracy is to build relationships with local officials and service providers. While it's important to maintain professional boundaries, getting to know the staff at your local municipality office, post office, or bank can often smooth the way for future interactions. Italians generally appreciate personal relationships and may be more inclined to go the extra mile to help someone they know.

Language can be a significant barrier when navigating Italian bureaucracy. While English is widely spoken in tourist areas and larger cities, many official procedures are conducted exclusively in Italian. Even in offices that deal frequently with foreigners, such as immigration offices, you may find that staff have limited English proficiency. Therefore, investing time in learning Italian can be incredibly valuable. Not only will it help you in your day-to-day life, but it can also make bureaucratic processes much smoother. If you're not confident in your Italian skills, consider hiring a professional interpreter for important meetings or procedures.

Another important aspect of dealing with Italian bureaucracy is understanding the concept of "ufficio competente" or the competent office. In the Italian system, different offices or departments are responsible for specific tasks, and it's crucial to ensure you're dealing with the correct office for your particular need. Sometimes, you may find yourself being redirected from one office to another as you try to accomplish a task. While this can be frustrating, it's part of the system's structure to ensure that each matter is handled by the appropriate experts.

Patience is perhaps the most important virtue when dealing with Italian bureaucracy. Processes that might seem straightforward can often take much longer than expected. It's not uncommon for simple procedures to require multiple visits to an office or for processing times to extend well beyond initial estimates. It's important to build this potential for delays into your plans and to avoid leaving important tasks until the last minute.

One way to mitigate some of the stress of dealing with Italian bureaucracy is to take advantage of online services where available. In recent years, Italy has made significant strides in digitalizing many bureaucratic processes. For example, many tax-related procedures can now be completed online through the Agenzia delle Entrate website. Similarly, some municipalities offer online booking systems for appointments at various offices, which can save you time and frustration. However, it's important to note that the availability and sophistication of online services can vary greatly between different regions and municipalities.

Another strategy that many retirees find helpful is to create a well-organized system for managing documents and deadlines. Keep copies of all important documents, both physical and digital. Create a calendar system to track important dates, such as when various permits or certifications need to be renewed. Being proactive and organized can help you avoid last-minute rushes and potential penalties for missed deadlines.

It's also worth noting that bureaucratic processes can vary significantly between different regions and even individual municipalities in Italy. What works in one place may not be the same in another. This decentralization can be both a blessing and a curse. On one hand, it means that you may need to do some research to understand the specific procedures in your area. On the other hand, it can sometimes work to your advantage, as some regions or municipalities may have more streamlined or efficient processes than others.

One aspect of Italian bureaucracy that can be particularly challenging for retirees is dealing with banking and financial services. Opening a bank account in Italy, for example, can be a complex process involving numerous documents and verifications. You'll likely need to provide your passport, Codice Fiscale, proof of address, and potentially other documents depending on the bank's requirements. Some banks may also require you to demonstrate a certain level of Italian language proficiency.

Once you have a bank account, you may find that Italian banking practices differ from what you're used to. For example, checks are less commonly used in Italy than in some other countries, and there may be fees associated with various banking services that you might expect to be free. Understanding these differences and choosing a bank that caters to expatriates can help smooth your financial transitions.

Dealing with utilities is another area where you'll encounter bureaucracy. Setting up services like electricity, gas, water, and internet often involves complex contracts and multiple forms. You may need to provide your Codice Fiscale, proof of residency, and sometimes a deposit. It's not uncommon for the activation of these services to take longer than you might expect, so it's wise to start these processes well in advance of when you'll need the services.

One particularly Italian bureaucratic quirk that retirees often encounter is the "autocertificazione." This is a self-certification document where you declare certain facts about yourself under penalty of law. While this system was introduced to simplify some bureaucratic processes by reducing the need for official certificates, it can sometimes be confusing for foreigners who are not used to this level of self-declaration.

Despite the challenges, it's important to remember that millions of Italians and foreign residents successfully navigate these systems every day. With time and experience, you'll develop strategies for dealing with Italian bureaucracy more efficiently. Many retirees find that joining expat groups or online forums can be helpful, as these communities often share tips and experiences about dealing with various bureaucratic processes.

It's also worth noting that there are professional services available to help you navigate Italian bureaucracy. Many retirees choose to work with a commercialista (accountant) for tax matters, a geometra (surveyor) for property-related issues, and potentially a lawyer for more complex legal matters. While these services come at a cost, many find that the peace of mind and time saved are well worth the investment.

One final point to consider is the importance of maintaining a positive attitude when dealing with Italian bureaucracy. While it's easy to become frustrated with delays or seemingly illogical processes, maintaining a calm and courteous demeanor can go a long way. Italian officials are generally doing their best to help within the constraints of their systems, and a friendly approach can often lead to a more positive outcome.

In summary, navigating Italian bureaucracy is undoubtedly one of the more challenging aspects of retiring in Italy. It requires patience, persistence, and often a good sense of humor. However, with proper preparation, a willingness to learn, and perhaps a bit of help from professionals or experienced expats, you can successfully manage these systems. Remember that the bureaucratic hurdles are a small price to pay for the privilege of living in one of the world's most beautiful and culturally rich countries. By approaching these challenges with the right mindset, you'll be well on your way to fully enjoying your Italian retirement dream.

Chapter 10
Long-term Considerations

As you settle into your Italian retirement, it's crucial to look beyond the initial excitement and novelty of your new life and consider the long-term aspects of living in Italy. While the allure of sun-drenched piazzas, world-class cuisine, and rich cultural experiences may have drawn you to Italy, ensuring a sustainable and fulfilling retirement requires careful planning and consideration of various factors that will impact your life in the years to come. In this chapter, we'll explore these long-term considerations, from estate planning and healthcare to maintaining connections with your home country and adapting to the evolving needs of aging in a foreign land.

One of the most important long-term considerations for retirees in Italy is estate planning. While it may not be the most pleasant topic to contemplate, having a clear plan for your assets and final wishes is crucial, especially when living in a foreign country. Italian inheritance laws can be complex and may differ significantly from those in your home country. For example, Italy has forced heirship rules, which means that a certain portion of your estate must be left to close relatives, regardless of your wishes. This can be particularly important if you have children or a spouse and want to ensure they are provided for according to your intentions.

To navigate these complexities, it's highly advisable to consult with a legal professional who specializes in international estate planning. They can help you understand how Italian law interacts with the laws of your home country and guide you in creating a will that is valid and enforceable in both jurisdictions. In some cases, you may need to create separate wills for your Italian assets and those in your home country. It's also important to keep in mind that Italy has inheritance taxes, which can be substantial depending on the relationship between the deceased and the heir and the value of the assets inherited.

Another aspect of estate planning to consider is the designation of a power of attorney. This legal document allows you to appoint someone to make decisions on your behalf if you become incapacitated. In Italy, this is known as a "procura" and can be crucial in ensuring your affairs are managed according to your wishes if you're unable to do so yourself. It's particularly important to have this in place when living far from family members who might otherwise naturally step into this role.

Healthcare is another critical long-term consideration for retirees in Italy. While Italy's public healthcare system is generally of high quality and accessible to legal residents, it's important to think about how your healthcare needs might evolve as you age. Consider researching the availability of specialized medical services in your area, particularly for any chronic conditions you may have or be at risk for. Some retirees choose to maintain private health insurance in addition to their coverage under the Italian system, which can provide quicker access to certain treatments and a wider choice of healthcare providers.

It's also worth considering the availability of long-term care options in Italy. The concept of nursing homes or assisted living facilities is less common in Italy than in some other countries, with families tradition-ally taking on more responsibility for caring for elderly relatives. However, there are options available, including "case di riposo" (rest homes) and "residenze sanitarie assistenziali" (assisted healthcare residences). Researching these options in your area and understanding the costs and processes involved can help you plan for potential future needs.

Language considerations also play a crucial role in long-term health-care planning. While you may be able to get by with basic Italian for day-to-day life, medical situations often require a higher level of language proficiency. Consider investing time in improving your Italian language skills, particularly medical terminology. Some retirees also find it helpful to build relationships with English-speaking health-care providers or to identify translation services that can assist in medical situations.

Financial planning is another critical aspect of ensuring a sustainable retirement in Italy. While you may have carefully budgeted for your move and initial years in Italy, it's important to regularly review and adjust your financial plan. Consider factors such as inflation, exchange rate fluctuations (if you're receiving pension or investment income from another country), and potential changes in tax laws that could affect your financial situation.

It's also important to stay informed about changes in pension regulations, both in Italy and in your home country. Some countries have agreements with Italy regarding the payment and taxation of pensions, but these agreements can change over time. Regularly consulting with a financial advisor who understands both Italian and international finance can help you stay on top of these issues and make informed decisions about your retirement savings and investments.

Another financial consideration is the potential need for additional income in your later retirement years. While Italy can offer a lower cost of living than some other Western countries, unexpected expenses can arise, particularly related to healthcare or property maintenance. Some retirees find part-time work or freelance opportunities to supplement their income, while others may consider options like reverse mortgages (although these are less common in Italy than in some other countries). Understanding your options and planning for potential financial needs can help ensure your long-term financial stability.

Maintaining connections with your home country is another important long-term consideration. While you may be fully embracing your new life in Italy, keeping ties with your country of origin can be important for both practical and emotional reasons. From a practical standpoint, you may need to periodically renew documents like passports or driver's licenses, file tax returns, or manage property or investments in your home country. Setting up systems to handle these tasks efficiently, such as digital access to accounts and reliable mail forwarding services, can help you manage these responsibilities from afar.

Emotionally, maintaining connections with family and friends in your home country can be crucial for your long-term wellbeing. While technology has made it easier than ever to stay in touch, it's important to proactively maintain these relationships. Consider setting up regular video calls, planning visits (both to and from Italy), and finding ways to involve distant loved ones in your new life. Some retirees find it helpful to start a blog or social media account to share their experiences in Italy, which can be a great way to keep everyone updated and feeling connected.

It's also worth considering how you'll handle major life events that occur in your home country, such as weddings, births, or funerals. Having a plan in place for these situations, including setting aside funds for unexpected travel, can help you navigate these emotional times more easily.

As you think about the long term, it's important to consider how your needs and desires might change as you age. The charming hillside town that seemed perfect when you first retired might become challenging to navigate as you get older. The isolated countryside villa might feel less appealing if driving becomes difficult. When choosing where to settle in Italy, think not just about your current preferences, but about how well the location will suit you in 10 or 20 years.

Consider factors like the availability of public transportation, the proximity to healthcare facilities, and the ease of accessing daily necessities like groceries and pharmacies. Some retirees find that moving from a rural area to a smaller city as they age provides a good balance of Italian charm and practical amenities. Others might choose to live in an area popular with other expatriates, which can provide a built-in community and often easier access to English-speaking services.

It's also worth thinking about the type of housing that will suit you in the long term. While a multi-story home might be manageable now, consider whether it will still be practical as you age. Features like elevator access, walk-in showers, and minimal stairs can become increasingly important. If you're purchasing property, consider whether it can be easily adapted for aging in place, or whether you might need to plan for a future move.

Another long-term consideration is building and maintaining a support network in Italy. While the initial years of retirement might be filled with travel and new experiences, having a strong local community becomes increasingly important as time goes on. This can include both expatriate and Italian friends, as well as connections with neighbors, local shopkeepers, and service providers.

Engaging in community activities, joining clubs or associations, or volunteering can be great ways to build these connections. Many retirees find that becoming involved in local issues or cultural preservation efforts helps them feel more rooted in their adopted community. Learning the local dialect, if different from standard Italian, can also help you connect more deeply with your neighbors and feel more at home in your area.

It's also important to think about how you'll stay mentally and physically active in the long term. While Italy offers plenty of opportunities for an active lifestyle, it's easy to fall into routines that might not provide enough stimulation or exercise. Consider how you'll challenge yourself mentally, whether through learning new skills, engaging in creative pursuits, or continuing education. Many Italian universities offer programs for mature students, which can be a great way to keep learning and meet like-minded people.

Physical activity is equally important for healthy aging. While walking through Italian towns and villages can provide good everyday exercise, consider how you might maintain a more structured fitness routine. This could involve joining a gym, taking up swimming, or participating in group activities like hiking clubs or dance classes. Not only will this help maintain your health, but it can also be a great way to socialize and stay connected to your community.

As you age, you may also need to consider how to adapt your travel and leisure activities. While you may currently enjoy frequent trips around Italy and Europe, mobility issues or health concerns might make this more challenging in the future. Think about how you can continue to enjoy new experiences and cultural enrichment even if your ability to travel becomes limited. This might involve exploring local events and attractions more deeply, engaging in armchair travel through books and films, or using technology to virtually visit museums and landmarks around the world.

Technology itself is an important long-term consideration. As digital services become increasingly integral to daily life, staying up-to-date with technology can help you maintain independence and stay connected. This might involve learning to use smartphones and tablets, becoming comfortable with online banking and shopping, or using telehealth services. Many Italian communities offer courses specifically designed to help older adults navigate new technologies, which can be a great way to learn these skills while also socializing.

Another aspect to consider is how you'll manage home maintenance and daily tasks as you age. The charming old Italian home that seems like a wonderful project in your early retirement years might become a burden later on. Think about how you'll handle tasks like gardening, cleaning, and home repairs in the long term. Some retirees find it helpful to budget for household help or to gradually adapt their home to be lower maintenance.

It's also important to think about transportation in the long term. While you might currently enjoy driving around the Italian countryside, there may come a time when this is no longer feasible or desirable. Research public transportation options in your area and consider how well they would serve your needs if you were no longer able to drive. Some retirees choose to live in town centers where most daily needs can be met on foot, while others might plan to use taxis or car services more frequently as they age.

Climate is another factor to consider for the long term. While Italy's climate is generally mild, some areas can experience extreme heat in summer or cold in winter. As you age, you might find you're more sensitive to temperature extremes. Think about how well your home can be heated or cooled, and consider whether you might want to travel during the most extreme months. Some retirees adopt a pattern of spending winters in warmer coastal areas and summers in cooler hill towns.

One of the more difficult long-term considerations is planning for end-of-life care and arrangements. While it's not a pleasant topic, having a clear plan can provide peace of mind and reduce stress for you and your loved ones. This includes not only legal and financial arrangements, as discussed earlier, but also personal preferences for care and funeral arrangements. Italy has its own customs and regulations regarding end-of-life matters, which may differ from those in your home country. Researching these and making your wishes known to both your Italian contacts and your family in your home country can help ensure your preferences are respected.

It's also worth considering how you'll handle major global events or crises from your position as an expatriate retiree in Italy. The COVID-19 pandemic, for example, highlighted the importance of having contingency plans for unexpected situations. This might include having a plan for if you need to return to your home country quickly, understanding your rights and options for healthcare in crisis situations, and ensuring you have adequate emergency funds easily accessible.

Retiring to Italy

Another long-term consideration is how you'll continue to grow and find purpose in your retirement years. While the first few years might be filled with the excitement of exploring your new home, it's important to think about how you'll continue to find fulfillment in the longer term. This might involve setting new goals for yourself, whether learning a craft, writing a book, or mastering the art of Italian cooking. Many retirees find that sharing their skills and experiences, whether through teaching, mentoring, or volunteering, provides a sense of purpose and connection to their community.

It's also important to consider how you'll handle transitions in your social circle over time. As an expatriate retiree, you might find that your social group is more fluid than it would be in your home country, with friends potentially moving away or returning to their home countries. Cultivating a diverse social network and being open to forming new friendships can help ensure you maintain a strong support system over the years.

Staying informed about both Italian and international news and developments is another important long-term consideration. As a resident of Italy, you'll be affected by Italian political and economic developments, but you may also need to stay abreast of changes in your home country that could affect your pension, investments, or legal status. Consider how you'll access reliable news sources in both Italian and your native language, and think about joining expatriate organizations that can help keep you informed about issues affecting foreign residents in Italy.

Finally, it's crucial to periodically reassess your decision to retire in Italy and be open to the possibility that your needs or desires might change over time. While many retirees find that Italy becomes more beloved to them as the years pass, others might find that they want to be closer to family or that they miss aspects of their home culture. Having a "plan B" – whether that's returning to your home country, moving to a different part of Italy, or even exploring a new country – can provide peace of mind and flexibility as your life evolves.

This might involve maintaining a property or investments in your home country, staying informed about retirement options in other locations, or simply remaining open to the idea that your ideal retirement situation might change over time. Remember that there's no shame in deciding to make a change if your current situation no longer suits you – the goal is to ensure that your retirement years are as fulfilling and comfortable as possible, wherever that might be.

In summary, while retiring in Italy offers a wealth of wonderful experiences and opportunities, ensuring a successful long-term retirement requires careful consideration and planning. From estate planning and healthcare to maintaining connections with your home country and adapting to the changing needs of aging, there are many factors to consider. By thinking through these long-term considerations and regularly reassessing your plans, you can help ensure that your Italian retirement continues to be fulfilling and enjoyable for years to come. Remember, the goal is not just to retire in Italy, but to thrive there, embracing all that this beautiful country has to offer while also planning prudently for the future. With thoughtful preparation and an open mind, your Italian retirement can truly be a rich and rewarding chapter of your life, full of discovery, growth, and joy.

Afterword
Embracing La Dolce Vita (The Sweet Life)

As we come to the end of our journey through "Retiring in Italy: The Complete Guide to Living Your Italian Dream" it's time to reflect on the path we've traveled together and the adventures that lie ahead. Throughout this book, we've explored the myriad facets of Italian life that make it such an enticing retirement destination, from its sun-drenched landscapes and rich cultural heritage to its world-renowned cuisine and welcoming communities. We've also delved into the practical considerations and potential challenges of making this dream a reality, arming you with the knowledge and insights you need to embark on your own Italian retirement adventure.

The allure of retiring in Italy is as multifaceted as the country itself. It's a land where history breathes through every stone, where art isn't confined to museums but spills out onto the streets, and where the pursuit of beauty and pleasure is woven into the fabric of daily life. Italy offers a lifestyle that prioritizes quality over quantity, human connection over material accumulation, and living in the moment over constantly rushing toward the future. It's a place where you can wake up each morning to the aroma of freshly baked bread, spend your days exploring centuries-old villages or lounging on Mediterranean beaches, and end each evening with a leisurely meal shared with friends old and new.

We began our exploration by dreaming of Italy, considering the various regions and what they offer to retirees. From the sun-baked hills of Tuscany to the dramatic coastlines of Sicily, from the fashion-forward streets of Milan to the timeless canals of Venice, we discovered that Italy offers a diverse array of settings to suit every taste and lifestyle. Whether you're drawn to the bustling energy of city life, the tranquility of the countryside, or the laid-back rhythm of coastal living, Italy has a place that can feel like home.

As we delved into the practicalities of making your Italian retirement a reality, we navigated the sometimes complex waters of legal requirements and bureaucratic processes. We explored the various visa options available to retirees, the steps involved in obtaining residency permits, and the documentation needed to establish your new life in Italy. While these processes can sometimes seem daunting, we've provided you with the knowledge and strategies to approach them with confidence, understanding that each successfully completed form brings you one step closer to your dream.

Financial considerations formed a crucial part of our discussion, as we examined the costs of living in different parts of Italy and strategies for managing your finances across international borders. We explored the Italian tax system, banking practices, and options for healthcare coverage, giving you the tools to create a solid financial foundation for your retirement. We also looked at the potential for stretching your retirement savings further in Italy, where many find they can enjoy a higher quality of life for less than in their home countries.

Finding the perfect home in Italy was another key topic, as we explored the pros and cons of renting versus buying, the intricacies of the Italian property market, and the joys and challenges of restoring a centuries-old property. We journeyed through the sun-drenched farmhouses of Tuscany, the charming apartments in medieval hill towns, and the seaside villas of the Italian Riviera, helping you envision where your own Italian story might unfold.

Healthcare is always a primary concern for retirees, and we took a deep dive into the Italian healthcare system, renowned for its quality and accessibility. We explored how to register for the national health service, the options for private insurance, and the availability of specialized care. We also touched on the Italian approach to wellness and preventive care, which aligns well with many retirees' focus on maintaining health and vitality in their golden years.

One of the most exciting aspects of retiring in Italy is the opportunity to immerse yourself in a new culture and way of life. We discussed strategies for overcoming language barriers, building social connections, and truly becoming part of your new community. From joining local clubs and associations to participating in town festivals and events, we explored the many ways you can weave yourself into the social fabric of your new home.

Daily life in Italy formed another important part of our exploration. We delved into the rhythms and customs that make Italian life unique, from the morning ritual of espresso at the local bar to the evening passeggiata through town. We explored the joys of shopping in local markets, the etiquette of dining out in Italy, and the pleasures of embracing a more relaxed pace of life. These daily experiences, we discovered, are often where the true magic of Italian life reveals itself.

Italy's unparalleled cultural riches offer endless opportunities for exploration and personal growth in retirement. We journeyed through world-class museums and galleries, walked in the footsteps of ancient Romans, and lost ourselves in medieval hill towns frozen in time. We also explored the many opportunities for active pursuits, from hiking in the Dolomites to cycling through the Tuscan countryside, proving that retirement in Italy can be as active and adventurous as you wish to make it.

Afterword

Throughout our journey, we've been honest about the challenges that come with retiring in a foreign country. We've tackled head-on the frustrations of dealing with Italian bureaucracy, the potential for culture shock, and the difficulties of being far from family and familiar support systems. But we've also provided strategies for overcoming these challenges, emphasizing the importance of patience, flexibility, and a sense of humor in navigating your new life.

As we looked to the long-term future, we considered how your needs and desires might evolve over time. We explored options for accessing support services as you age, strategies for staying connected with loved ones back home, and the importance of estate planning in an international context. Through it all, we emphasized the importance of remaining open to new experiences and continuing to embrace the joy of discovery that brought you to Italy in the first place.

Now, as we close the final chapter of this book, it's important to remember that this is really just the beginning of your journey. The true adventure begins when you take these insights and information and apply them to your own unique circumstances and dreams. Retiring in Italy is not a one-size-fits-all proposition – it's a deeply personal journey that will be shaped by your own preferences, experiences, and the unexpected twists and turns that life inevitably brings.

Remember that while careful planning is essential, it's equally important to remain open to the serendipitous moments and unexpected joys that often become the most treasured memories. Perhaps it's a conversation with a local shopkeeper that blossoms into a lifelong friendship, a wrong turn while exploring that leads you to a breathtaking view you never knew existed, or a local festival that immerses you in centuries-old traditions. These unplanned moments are often where the true magic of Italian life reveals itself.

As you embark on this new chapter of your life, carry with you the spirit of adventure and openness that brought you to this point. Embrace the challenges as opportunities for growth, savor the daily

Afterword

pleasures that Italian life offers in abundance, and allow yourself to be transformed by the beauty, history, and warmth of your new home.

Retiring in Italy is more than just a change of address – it's an opportunity to reimagine your life, to challenge yourself in new ways, and to discover facets of yourself that may have remained dormant in more familiar surroundings. It's a chance to slow down and savor life's moments, to prioritize experiences over possessions, and to build deep, meaningful connections with a new community and culture.

Whether you find yourself sipping espresso in a sun-drenched piazza, getting lost in the winding streets of a medieval town, perfecting your pasta-making skills in a Tuscan farmhouse kitchen, or simply watching the sun set over the Mediterranean, remember that you are not just observing Italian life – you are living it. You are writing your own chapter in Italy's long and storied history.

So, as you close this book and look toward the horizon of your own Italian adventure, do so with excitement, with courage, and with an open heart. The path ahead may not always be smooth, but it promises to be endlessly rewarding. Embrace the spirit of la dolce vita – the sweet life – in all its complexity and beauty. Your Italian retirement adventure awaits, filled with the promise of new experiences, deep connections, and the joy of living life to its fullest.

Buona fortuna e buon viaggio – good luck and bon voyage – on your journey into the heart of Italian life. May your retirement years be filled with the warmth of Italian sunshine, the richness of Italian culture, and the deep satisfaction of a life well-lived. Benvenuti alla vostra nuova vita italiana – welcome to your new Italian life.